# DREAM BACK YOUR LIFE

# DREAM BACK YOUR LIFE

## A Practical Guide to Dreams, Daydreams, and Fantasies

Joan Mazza, M.S.

A PERIGEE BOOK

A Perigee Book
Published by The Berkley Publishing Group
A division of Penguin Putnam Inc.
375 Hudson Street
New York, New York 10014

First edition: July 2000

Published simultaneously in Canada.

The Penguin Putnam Inc. World Wide Web site address is
http://www.penguinputnam.com

Library of Congress Cataloging-in-Publication Data

Mazza, Joan.
    Dream back your life : a practical guide to dreams, daydreams, and fantasies / Joan
Mazza.—1st ed.
        p. cm.
    Includes index.
    ISBN 0-399-52610-2
    1. Dreams. 2. Fantasy. 3. Self-realization. I. Title.

BF1099.S36 M39 2000
154.6'3—dc21

                                                                                00-027431

Printed in the United States of America

10  9  8  7  6  5  4  3  2  1

For all the members and friends of
Twin Oaks Community*—
my constant teachers

* Twin Oaks Community is an intentional egalitarian community of approximately eighty adults and fifteen children on 460 acres in central Virginia, established in 1967. For more information, go to *http://www.twinoaks.org/*.

# CONTENTS

## PART TWO
# Waking Dreams

## PART THREE
# Dreaming Your Future

# ACKNOWLEDGMENTS

THIS book has evolved over many years of my own development and education. Much of that growth would never have happened without my good friends who continue to teach and encourage me.

As always, my first thank-you is to Joyce Sweeney, sister-writer, who read the first drafts of this manuscript when they were at their most raw. Thank you for telling me with humor and love when my writing was word salad: "re-toss this salad," "some lettuce here," "lots of salad, but very nutritious ingredients." You have been so much help, such a good teacher, and a wonderful role model. So many of our conversations became part of this book. I am at a loss for words to fully express my gratitude!

---

MORE thanks go to the following people:

Heidi Boehringer, for reading the completed first draft and making excellent suggestions, in spite of a very busy writing life of your own.

Naomi Seijo, for being willing to make the time and energy to read the manuscript and make comments.

Dianne Grandstrom of Twin Oaks Community, for raising important questions about freedom, autonomy, and labels.

Joan McIver, for the final title after this book's many incarnations during Joyce's Thursday writing group.

My nephew Justin Coppolino, for keeping my printers and copier running, supplying me with refills, and encouraging me to tackle printer repairs without fear.

My nephew Eric Francis, for our many provocative and thought-provoking conversations.

My yoga teacher, Jimmy Barkan, at the Yoga College of India in Fort Lauderdale, whose teaching continues to support my writing; body discipline carries over into a healthy mind.

My psychodrama trainers, Nina Garcia and Dale Richard Buchanan, for their wonderful example of professional and compassionate work.

Jake Kawatski, Alexandra McGee, and Carolina Small, for their permission to use their mission statements.

My many supportive fellow writers, colleagues, and dreamers: Suzanne Anderson, Lois Avrick, Norma Berkman, Mary Beth Busutil, Lera Chacón, Naomi Childers, Carol Collins, Gene Cryer, Daniel Deluca, Brenda Diaz, Betty Dodson, Elinor Eckart, Lynn Edinoff, Gloria Fisher, Larry Fleischman, Alexandra Flinn, Golda Freundlich, Art Germain, Myra Gross, Virginia Havens, Anthousa Helena, Christian Henz, Jay Johnson, Rosemary Jones, Lesley Kleiner, Barbara Lange, Michele Lessirard, Marj Lyons, Mary Mastin, Kathleen McCaslin, Richard Nathanson, Jack Nease, Renee Ninov, Arnie Perlstein, Susan Platzer, Elise Pouliot, Bill Rea, Gloria Rothstein, Lana Schulman, Mimi Shapiro, Lucille Shulklapper, Edith Sloan, Mark Dennis Smith, Cher Souci, Gale St. John, Mel Standen, Liz Sterling, Mel Taylor, Noreen Wald, Larry Ward, Archie Wilson, Sherri Winston, Sally Yates, and Jennie Zeiner.

My agent, Lori Perkins, for being as enthusiastic as I am about my writing, and for finding venues for its publication.

My editor, Sheila Curry, at Perigee, whose suggestions and corrections made this a much more cogent and cohesive book.

---

ANY muddles that remain are my own.

# INTRODUCTION

EVERYONE dreams.

Every night, we enter the world of our dreams, whether we remember our dreams or not. While we're awake, we dream, too. We spin our fantasies and hopes, and we plan our futures.

This book is about both kinds of dreams—waking and sleeping—and how they point us toward our futures. Our dreams tell us who we really are, how to live more authentically, and how to find and live our true purpose. They contain solutions to our problems and a more honest evaluation of our life choices and actions.

This is a book about making friends with your mind. You have many different thoughts and feelings across the spectrum of consciousness, from deep sleep to full, waking, alert awareness. The discussions and exercises in this book suggest that you observe these different mental and emotional processes with the spirit of adventure and the curiosity of an explorer.

No one can tell you how to live or what is best for you. This book is a guide to help you find your own way back to yourself—to those parts of yourself that you have lost, ignored, denied, or shelved because you believed you had to let them go. If you have had enough of mediocrity, just coasting, or a general sense of malaise in your life, if you believe something more awaits you, then you are ready for what you will find in the pages ahead—to dream back your life.

This book will help you focus on solutions instead of problems. You will learn to trust that you have your own answers, and that you are the expert on what you need to do. The underlying philosophy is to find what works for you and to do it more often and consistently.

In my earlier book, *Dreaming Your Real Self: A Personal Approach to Dream Interpretation,* I mapped out the basic principles and techniques of remembering and understanding the meaning of your dreams and nightmares. This book takes those basic methods to the next level—taking the insights of your waking and sleeping dreams into action in your life.

When a dream says you are being unnecessarily fearful or cautious, you can take those *dream meanings* into *action.* When a dream encourages you, tells you that you are doing well, and shows you your bliss, you can move toward it. By tuning in to your dream messages, you can bring your life more into harmony with your deepest needs and wants.

———

PART One of this book explores the nature of nighttime dreams, particularly nightmares and pivotal dreams. Dramatic dreams can frequently point the way to changes and the strategies for making them, or to the resolution of an important problem. This section of the book also discusses ways to intentionally use night dreams to discover answers to our problems. By understanding dream signposts and recurring metaphors, and by incubating or programming dreams for assistance with specific questions, we can find solutions.

Part Two discusses the variety of daydreams, including fantasies, self-talk, visualization, and our childhood expectations and how they can reveal a more authentic self that we may have lost sight of during our busy, practical, adult lives. What we might have considered only idle thinking takes on a new level of meaning and productive potential.

Part Three focuses on steps and strategies for finding your purpose and mission in life. By writing a mission statement and getting clear on what you want to accomplish, your visions can move from vague ideas into purposeful action. This section examines a variety of motivational techniques to get on track to living your own unique and authentic path.

At the end of each chapter are "Dreams into Action" exercises—a way to actively engage you in the ideas you read, to have you participate more than intellectually. The action of writing your answers to the questions is the beginning of taking steps to dream back your life.

I encourage you to write in the margins, underline and cross out, highlight and argue with the ideas. Do make comments in the book and in your journal to express your criticism and disagreement, as well as your praise and your significant moments of insight and personal awareness. The more strongly you react, the more you can discover about the meanings you make in your life. Forceful responses (positive or negative) tell you a lot about yourself, and paying attention to them can be very helpful. Writing them can offer insights.

While you are reading this book, make note of your nighttime dreams and write them in your journal. Powerful information lies in your unconscious. Understanding these messages is important if you are to make changes in your life.

Because keeping a journal comes up so often in the exercises and discussions in this book, I suggest you purchase a notebook or blank book for this purpose and plan to write as often as you like.

## Tips for Keeping a Journal

1. Write every day, preferably at the same time of day.

2. Record your dreams alongside your day's events.

3. Find a way to secure your journal to feel confident that its contents are private.

4. Do not share your journal with others.

5. Write about your feelings, concerns, deepest passions, and hopes—not just events.

6. Question your assumptions, perceptions, righteous indignations, and underlying beliefs.

7. Give your dark side permission to have its say.

8. Do not censor yourself.

9. Don't worry about punctuation, spelling, or format.

10. Make lists and charts of your life and plans.

11. Reread occasionally to acknowledge how far you have progressed (or to find the places where you are still stuck).

12. Use the journal to record your creative ideas. You may want to consider carrying a small journal or notebook with you at all times for ideas and thoughts you want to write more about at a later time.

13. Draw or doodle in your journal.

14. Notice patterns and repetitions and how they might be opportunities for making changes.

15. If this were someone else's journal, what would it reveal about their character and potential?

PART ONE

# Sleeping Dreams

# CHAPTER ONE

# How Dreaming Can Help You Take Back Your Life

If a little dreaming is dangerous, the cure for it is not to dream less but to dream more, to dream all the time.
—Marcel Proust

The unique value of dreams for our waking life rests on the fact that we do something asleep and dreaming that we cannot do nearly as well while awake. We look at ourselves with greater honesty and in greater depth.
—Montague Ullman

WHAT does it mean to *dream back your life?*

Most people, at some time or another, have the feeling that along life's path they have lost their way. Maybe you have achieved some success and are doing well, but you have a nagging feeling that something is missing. This book offers methods that you can use to find your true path or your way back to your authentic self. When people hear the phrase, "take back your life," they seem to sit up and listen.

The authentic self is who you were before you were socialized by a culture, an era, and an ethnic and religious group. The authentic self contains your talents and gifts that you were born with, before they were corrected out of you by your family's desire to raise a "civilized child" who would fit into society. When you are living authentically, you have a confident center and no longer have to pretend to be someone you are not.

What is it you feel you need to take back? Is it lost forever or just misplaced? How can you identify what's missing?

Whether you feel you have given your life away or someone took it from you, this book will help you reclaim your authentic self and the life you want to live. Regardless of what you may perceive as constraints and obstacles (age, gender, money, obligations, responsibilities, and so on), you *can* dream back your life.

Sometimes dreams, whether they are waking fantasies or full-blown nightmares, give you information that shakes you up. You may find yourself dreaming or fantasizing about things that disturb you. These are often the very images that can catapult you into the next stage of your personal evolution—if you are willing to open yourself to these images and implement the dream message into life action. These signs in visions, daydreams, and nighttime phantasms contain the seeds of your growth. When you learn to see and comprehend these signs, they can change your life. By looking at their messages, you can understand how they are signposts and directions for your future. By considering them as pivotal events and taking action, you can save yourself from wasted steps, wrong turns, and detours on your life's journey.

## FUNCTIONS OF DREAMING

Dreaming, whether awake or asleep, has many functions. We dream as a way of keeping ourselves together to live with more happiness. Both our night dreams and daydreams help us to do the following:

- Solve problems—by mulling over a problem in dreams, we produce a variety of solutions, see the problem from different points of view, and find a resolution to the issue.

* Clarify our plans—we develop strategies, steps, and safety nets for accomplishing our goals.

* Process and clarify feelings—we experience the full range and variety of our emotions and are able to step outside them for better clarity.

* Sort out our innermost thoughts and ideas—in the safety and privacy of our own minds, we have the full range of mental processing that we might not share with others.

* Express to ourselves what we believe we cannot express to others—we ventilate our thoughts and feelings safely and without fear of consequences.

* Evaluate risks and consequences—dreams help us see the folly or wisdom of our future actions.

* Motivate ourselves to achieve a goal—by imagining a goal accomplished, we are inspired to persist and overcome obstacles.

* Consolidate learning—dreams provide a mental review and clarification of newly learned skills and information.

* Practice new behaviors (mental modeling)—by imagining ourselves already doing something we want to do, dreaming helps us to mentally practice the action and make it more comfortable to do these new behaviors in reality.

* Anticipate our future—we hope and plan for a future with greater vision and clarity to make it come about as we want it to be.

* Give ourselves needed pleasure and satisfaction—our dreams and fantasies soothe us and satisfy us when we need them or when we cannot perform the actions in life due to the constraints of reality.

- Review and learn from our mistakes—we mentally play back the tapes of unsatisfactory conversations, events, and blunders so that we can sort out how we can conduct ourselves differently in the future.

- Tap into our creativity—daydreams and night dreams come from the same source as all of our creativity. Having access to dreams means we can access our creative wellspring.

- See our present circumstances in the context of our whole lives—in dreams and fantasies, we see ourselves in the bigger picture of all that we can and want to be.

- Consider the quality of our relationships and how we might improve them—we examine their strengths and weaknesses and get direction for refining them.

- Center and stabilize ourselves emotionally—we gain greater peace and serenity through dreaming.

- Reveal unconscious processes—we have access to deeper layers of consciousness that can facilitate our personal evolution, however we comprehend it.

## My Dream

*I am going to be executed later in the day by lethal injection at a local hospital.*

*In the dream, I am in a kitchen in what feels like a vacation home. My parents are with me, alive and well, as they might have looked in the early 1980s. I am not lucid in the dream and I am not aware that my parents are both already dead. My mother is cooking and I'm talking with my father. I am thinking seriously about my impending death, but I am not at all afraid. Nor do I feel there is any injustice here. I don't know why I'm being executed, but it seems appropriate. It's inevitable, but not really a big deal. My true feelings are under the surface. I am pondering whom to tell and whom not to tell about my dying. Should this be a secret? This seems too important to ignore. I am feeling as if I see everything through this lens of having only a few hours left. But everything seems trivial—material things, worries, and concerns.*

*At one point, I say to my mother with great anguish, "This is the last day of my life!" She seems to feel for me, but it's not enough to comfort me in my distress. I don't really feel understood.*

*My main concern in the dream is how to spend the balance of the time I have left. I ask my father when we have to be at the hospital and he says six-thirty. It's about lunchtime, so I know I have six hours left. I am thinking that I should probably clean out my office and save the Flip-Frames from my overheads so they won't go to waste. I think of all the things I might sort through in my papers, but this seems like a huge job and definitely a waste of the very limited and precious time I have left.*

*My mother is making homemade pizza, but no one even asked me what I'd want for my last meal. I realize that she is doing this out of love, thinking she is pleasing me by making her special pizza, which she knows I like. But I'm also thinking that I want to go out to a very fancy restaurant, somewhere I wouldn't go otherwise. I know we can afford it, but I also know my parents won't want to spend the money. This is disheartening, but I am resigned to their choice.*

When I woke from this dream, I was immediately disturbed. Although I'm well aware that dreams are not prophecies in the way that most people fear, and that dreams about death are usually metaphors for something else, I had some concern about what the literal interpretation of this dream might be. I had some health concerns, but nothing dramatic or life threatening.

What struck me was that in the dream, I wasn't concerned about dying, but rather about using the time I had left. The dream's focus was on spending time and money.

The dream made it clear to me that I wasn't happy with how I was spending my time. I had a small view of my life of daily chores and not much adventure. For some time, I'd been feeling as if I needed a change. Time for something different instead of shuffling papers and worrying about money. My parents had trouble spending, depriving themselves right up until the end. They hadn't really been able to enjoy what they had worked so hard to accumulate. To me, the dream was a warning that my time, like theirs, was limited and that I should be enjoying it more. The dream seemed to say, "Don't be like your parents were."

These meanings were not immediately apparent, but I had a strong sense that this was a Big Dream, even if I wasn't sure what all the layers of meaning were.

Two days later, without having spent a lot of time on the dream, I went with my friend Gale to hear Richard Leakey speak about the plight of the African elephant. During the drive, Gale handed me a brochure for an African safari. Acting totally out of character from my usual cautious self, and without looking at any more than the cover of the brochure, I said, "I'll go with you." Gale hadn't even invited me and I wasn't sure she was planning a trip. She might have only been collecting information for the screenplay she was writing. When I spoke, I didn't know how long or when the trip would be, how much it cost, and whether I could get someone to stay with my dogs, always my first consideration for any travel. And yet I knew that there was a connection to my dream because of the next thing I said: "Life is too short; I'll go to Africa with you."

Gale was on the same page. A man in her office had died the week before of a massive heart attack. He was the same age as she. He never got his pension. He never got to enjoy what he had saved for his retirement. Another woman in her office was dying of cancer.

Having lived too much like my parents in fear of not having enough security, I was afraid that like them, I wasn't really living at all. At least I knew that my life could be richer and fuller than it had been. Only my fear had been in the way. And I'd better get moving and jump into my life with both feet before I ran out of time.

———————

FOR me, this dream and the decision to go to Africa came from the same place. Yes, some of the analysis and understanding of the dream came in hindsight, but I believe that's how it works. Dreams offer information about our process and our progress. We are always on the cusp of the next stage of our unfolding and maturity. Dreams, if we listen to them, can show us what the next stage is and they can help take us there. They can provide the pivotal moments in our lives to propel us into our most positive future.

## PERSONAL CORE ISSUES

Each of us has core issues that we deal with throughout our lives. We can recognize a core issue when we find ourselves in similar circumstances again and again. These may involve dealing with a particular kind of difficult person—perhaps with a family member as the prototype. We may be faced repeatedly with similar challenges of health or endurance, or having to come to terms with certain challenges of relationships. We may struggle with intimacy versus connection or problems with authority and control. Of course, we all have to deal with variations on these dilemmas. But for some, a particular trial seems to come up regularly. These core issues will frequently be the subject of our dreams, even those that are triggered by events at the time of the dream. We each seem to have a global or core issue that we spend our lives trying to resolve.

In my dream, not only the immediate concerns of aging, time, and money are presented, but also some of my core issues around these subjects. The dream reflects my ongoing struggle throughout my life to shed the values of my family of origin and live my own life in my own way. In part, these are issues about pleasing those I love versus pleasing myself, not wanting to cause an upset, but needing to feel authentic and get my needs met.

In various forms, core issues continue to surface—with friends, lovers, co-workers, and even casual contacts with strangers. People who marry multiple times may discover the same core issues in each relationship.

Here are some core issues that other people have listed:

- A pervasive problem with authority figures; disliking being told what to do by anyone

- A feeling of being owned or controlled by others

- Fear that their natural emotions will drive others away

- An inability to commit to something or follow through beyond an enthusiastic beginning

- Holding on to the expectations that they will be abandoned by those they love

- Accepting responsibility for others instead of allowing them to be responsible for themselves

- Fear that their personal successes will alienate members of their family

- A hidden belief that people who are financially secure are greedy and shallow

Perhaps you already have an idea of what your core issues are. If you do, you will have the opportunity through this book to deal with them more effectively. Take a few moments now to jot down your core issues.

## FUTURE PROJECTION

The future can be what you create for yourself. To take a look into your future potential, I suggest you do the following meditation. You might want to tape-record it and play it back to yourself or have someone else read it aloud to you. Pause at least ten seconds between questions.

If you do the meditation while reading, you might want to close your eyes after each question and then make notes before going on to the next one. At the end of the meditation, do a journal entry to capture your thoughts and insights. You may want to do this meditation several times during the course of reading this book and over the next few months.

Remove distractions (children, pets, radio, television) or remove yourself from them to a place where you won't be interrupted or jarred by noise, movement, or requests from others.

Get comfortable. Sit upright in a comfortable chair with your feet flat on the floor. If your feet don't reach the floor flat and comfortably without pressure on the backs of your thighs, then use a pillow to support your feet. You may sit cross-legged on the floor or on a meditation cushion if that's comfortable.

Relax your body and your mind. Breathe deeply and allow the tension to drain from your body. You are going to peek into your future and allow your future-self to give your today-self advice and guidance.

Take three long, slow, deep breaths.

Imagine you are thirty years older than you are today. No matter what this age is, imagine that your future-self is healthy and articulate and can speak to your today-self. Imagine this future-self having thirty years' experience, wisdom, and knowledge of what choices worked and what didn't.

What does your future-self spontaneously say to you?

Future-self, what advice can you give me about my present life choices?

Ask your future-self a question.

What does it answer?

Remember that your future-self has the benefit of hindsight. It knows all you've been through.

What can you say about my life?

What can you say about what I didn't do these last thirty years?

What can you tell me about my fears and worries?

Tell me about the obstacles I have created for myself.

How can I face these challenges today?

How can I use these perceived obstacles to my advantage?

What do you want me to know *now*?

What steps can I take to set myself on better ground for the satisfying future that awaits me?

After you have completed this meditation and dialog with your future-self, record your thoughts and feelings in your personal journal.

Look over your notes and see what you'd like to add. You may want to read these before bedtime, and ask your unconscious to send you more information in a dream.

Be prepared to write upon waking.

Expect to be enlightened by your dreams—whether you are conscious or sleeping.

CHAPTER TWO

# Pivotal Dreams

It takes a lot of courage to show your dreams to someone else.

—Erma Bombeck

## WHAT IS A PIVOTAL DREAM?

Also called Big Dreams by Carl Jung, *pivotal dreams* are those that come to us at turning points in our lives. We might intentionally ask for them by programming or incubating a dream (see Chapter 6) or they may come spontaneously and unbidden, sometimes to our horror and dismay. These are the dreams that shake us up, that stay with us for years, or whose imagery haunts us for days. We may be out of sorts for some time following a pivotal dream, disturbed by the images and by our inability to decipher what they mean. We may have a sense of warning or a feeling of impending doom. The dream seems to be conveying an important message, but we are unable to grasp its significance. Like smoke, it drifts away without substance, leaving only an unpleasant residue.

All dreams offer significant and useful information. Some come to us gently and subtly, but some come to us with special effects. These are the ones we are most likely to remember.

You might look upon any dream as pivotal and important, but the ones most likely to fall in this category are those that really capture your attention.

## SIGNS OF A PIVOTAL DREAM

- Extremely vivid images

- Bright, intense colors

- Strong and upsetting emotions such as grief, terror, great passion, or love

- Themes of death or dismemberment

- Personal or world catastrophes

- Danger or violence with gory images

- Monsters and aliens

- Tactile sensations, such as feeling something rough, smooth, or slimy

- Body pains

- Body movement (kinesthetic sensations), such as feeling as if you're upside down or plunging into an abyss

- Odors, especially those attached to specific memories

- Tastes

- Dialogue that seems very important to the dreamer, perhaps a warning or essential guidance

The key to a dream's pivotal quality is the impact it has on the dreamer. A dream that lingers on the mind for any reason may be such an important dream.

## EXAMPLES OF PIVOTAL DREAMS

One woman, Nancy,* told a dream she recognized as pivotal at the time of the dream.

### HOW DOES YOUR GARDEN GROW?

*I was in the house and our gardener, Mario, who is Cuban, was there. My husband wasn't at home. One section of the landscaping in front of the house was all dead and scraggly and full of weeds. I asked Mario to dig up the dead stuff in that section. After I went back into the house, it suddenly occurred to me that Mario didn't understand my instructions. I ran out and he hadn't understood. He was digging everything up, even though the garden was doing all right. I ran out and started to yell at him, "No, no! Stop. Don't do that!" At first, he didn't respond. But then he understood. Somehow it suddenly wasn't all dug up, but had been replanted. He got very indignant that I had reprimanded him for digging it all up. He was in a huff and was leaving. I said, "No, no. Wait a minute. Let me walk over here and see how it looks from a different perspective. Maybe it will look better." And sure enough, when I walked out onto the lawn and looked at it from the street level, it was doing beautifully. It was thriving. There were plants there I had never noticed before. I didn't know where he had gotten them, but I had a very positive feeling about it.*

*At first, I had the thought that he had replanted by taking some plants from one section and moving them to another. Maybe he had separated some plants, as you do with bulbs like daffodils. But there were definitely plants that had never been growing there before. I asked, "Where did you get these?" and he indicated that we had always had them. I hadn't seen them because they were planted someplace else or were in a different configuration.*

* All names and identifying details of dreamers have been changed to respect their privacy.

At the time of this dream, Nancy recognized that this was an important message, signaling a change. She was in her mid-sixties, continuing to struggle with adapting to a second marriage she'd been in for five years. She had married her husband after knowing him only six months and had been saying for some time, with anger and dismay, that he was a different man than the one she believed she'd married. He was rigid and narrow. The dream revealed to her a dramatic change in her attitude.

Nancy's spontaneous associations to daffodils were that they were harbingers of spring—a time of renewal, rebirth, and new opportunity. She was aware of her tendency to want to get rid of stuff that troubled her. The dream told her that if she saw her situation from a different perspective, she might see it more positively. She was intrigued by being reminded that there were positive aspects of her husband and herself that she might not have even known were there because she had been focused on *the dead stuff*. She acknowledged her tendency to see things as all bad or all good, instead of valuing differences and accepting imperfection. Her inclination to judge others harshly included beating herself up as well. She said, "My knee-jerk reactions end up bashing me in the chin." She appreciated this as a big insight. Additionally, she said she was probably attracted to her husband because, "He's as judgmental as I am. We're just judgmental about different things!"

When I asked her about the title that she had given the dream, she recited, "Mary, Mary, quite contrary, how does your garden grow?" In choosing the title, she had unconsciously recognized her own contrary nature, which she projected onto her husband. The irony of seeing him as a foreign gardener supported her waking criticisms of him as well. Though he was neither Cuban nor foreign-born, they came from different parts of the country and different ethnic groups. She saw him as being culturally very unlike herself and found she was frequently putting those differences down, and "beating him up," as she put it.

The dream left Nancy hopeful and encouraged to be more open to her husband. By her change in perspective, she felt more optimistic about the future of their relationship than she had in a long time. More important, she had a clear idea of how she might take the message of the dream into *action* in her treatment of herself and others.

———————

ANOTHER dreamer, Lisa, told a dream she had had more than twenty-five years earlier.

> *Lisa is taking care of her son, who is three years old. He is playing in the yard outside the house while she is inside the house, studying. In the dream, she thinks she should check on the child, but doesn't feel like getting up and interrupting her reading. She feels as if she's being a bad mother and this motivates her to get up and call for him. When she goes to shout for her son, she instead calls the name of her brother.*
> *This simple error is so shocking to her that she sits bolt upright in bed and wakes up.*

Lisa's immediate emotional and physical reactions told her this was a very important dream. Because of its emotional impact, she began to work on her relationship with her brother and with her son. She marked this dream as a turning point for her, setting her on a path toward mending these relationships. She began to see how her mother had made her responsible for her brother and put her in a position of mothering him when she had been only a child herself. Significantly, when her brother was her son's age, he had been injured in a childhood mishap for which Lisa felt responsible. Now that she was responsible for her own children, this old accident troubled her once more, despite her brother's complete recovery. The old guilt caused her to doubt her competence as a mother. Her child, at the time of the dream, was having night terrors, creating further concern about her ability to be a suitable mother. The dream also called up her old resentment of her brother and having to care for him when she wanted to do other things, just as she wanted to study at the time she was taking care of her son.

One of the outcomes of the dream was that Lisa saw how she was projecting her feelings about her brother onto her son—mixing them up instead of discerning the differences between them and in her relationship to each of them. She was able to do further psychological work on these family issues at the time of the dream. Telling the dream now, she was aware that other concerns remained—even twenty-five years after the dream. She could now look upon this dream as a reminder to take better care of herself—the child in herself—who still needed mothering. She also acknowledged some areas in her marriage that she felt needed attention because of problems in her original family.

Lisa refers to this dream as "the key that unlocked many problems."

---

ONCE when I was speaking, a woman told of having a recurrent dream of being in a group home or a school dormitory. The dreams varied a bit, but the recurrent element was that beds were being assigned and she always seemed to feel anxious about where she would end up. In the dream fragment she told, she takes a room in a dormitory with a roommate who chooses her bed first, and the woman winds up with the one that was left. I rephrased, "You have a chance to choose, but you let others choose first and you get what is left." I asked her what she might be saying to herself with this recurrent dream. She said, "That I am not making my own claim. That I am settling. That I am not asking for what I want." I reminded her that the dream addresses not only her pattern of behavior generally, but also some specific instance of how she did this just before having the dream. It was clear from this dreamer's face that this was a moment of insight, of personal revelation for her. I suggested she pay attention to when she has the dream and to what she did preceding it. This was an opportunity—a turning point—for her to gain awareness of how her own behavior or her passivity resulted in her getting less than satisfactory results in her life.

---

AT a workshop I led, a young woman raised her hand and asked why she kept having dreams of sex with dangerous men. She said the dreams were very exciting, but they disturbed her. I asked her, "What are you doing in your life that feels good and you enjoy it, but you know it's dangerous for you?" She opened her mouth and then closed it tightly. "Everything I do is like that. I live on the edge. I do a lot of dangerous things that are unhealthy for me."

This woman was in a treatment program for alcohol and drug abuse. The dream supported her efforts toward recovery—pointing out the pleasures as well as the risks of her dangerous lifestyle. This was clearly a big moment for this dreamer—one that she could take into action to continue on a healthier path. I suggested she make some notes in her recovery journal about the dream and what she thought she was telling herself with this metaphor.

---

WE all have pivotal dreams, but most often we ignore them. Perhaps the discomfort we feel in the face of their unusual images or strong emotions makes us want to put them aside as "mental flatulence," as Stephen King says. Those dreams that shock us or the ones that we think of as too weird are exactly those that we are inclined to dismiss. But weird dreams are most likely to be pivotal.

Here is a dream from Wendy, a woman in her forties. The dream came on the last night of a vacation with Mark, a man she'd been dating for more than a year.

## SACRIFICE AND DISAPPEARANCE FOR CHRISTOPHER REEVE

*In the dream, I feel as if I'm watching a movie. A young woman is telling a man, Christopher Reeve, that she has sacrificed herself so that he could have his true love. This other woman, his true love, is never in the scene. The sacrificing young woman tells him this very sweetly, gently, express-ing her love for him. He is quite amazed at her generosity and he seems very appreciative. This is all taking place in a setting that is medieval, with rough-hewn stone walls. There may be bars on the windows, like a dungeon. As she is just about finished speaking, an ancient religious icon appears in the air. It is gold-leafed, about eight inches in height, a figure that I know represents Christ, but it also has some kind of colorful design like a rainbow or concentric circles of color on the body of the piece. The icon passes through the stone wall to the outside and I think there is a sound and a flash of light. At that moment, in midsentence, the young woman disappears. I shout out in anguish and shock, but this feels more like I'm in a movie audience. I worry that I've attracted attention to myself. I find the woman's disappearance extremely disturbing, although I wouldn't call this dream a nightmare. The ending seems to be extreme and unsatisfying. And I am dismayed that this young woman could disappear without a trace so quickly and easily, even if it's by her own choice.*

This was so unlike the usual pattern for this dreamer that it had her attention for a long time. In a recent discussion, Wendy said, "I am still convinced it offers layers of meaning I have yet to penetrate."

On the first working of the dream, Wendy said, "In the dream, I am not an active participant, but more of an observer. The idea of doing something for a man's happiness seemed to be a dominant theme. At the time of the dream, I had been concerned about Mark's wishes versus mine. While I certainly hadn't been restricted by his wishes, I found it very encumbering to consider his needs every time I wanted a little time to myself or wanted to talk to others in the group we traveled with. All during the trip, I kept having the fantasy of going back to the hotel alone. I felt a real need to go inward, be quiet, work on my spiritual self, plan the next phase of my work, and write. Perhaps I was the one who felt as if I was sacrificing too much for a man."

Wendy continued, "It's interesting that the male is played by Christopher Reeve who has been paralyzed from the neck down since a horseback riding accident. He is a very good-looking man who used to be Superman in the movies. Now he is seriously handicapped. Perhaps this is my feeling about Mark: an awareness of his handicaps that sometimes seem like paralysis. Whenever I ask him a question, even a simple one, it takes him so long to answer that it's maddening. It is this that makes me feel like he's slowing me down or dragging me down and I want to get away from him and do things at my own pace."

Wendy examined her dream using the Gestalt technique, which entails identifying with and speaking from the first person perspective for each of the images of the dream.

The elements:

1. Woman who sacrifices herself

2. Christopher Reeve

3. Christian icon

4. Stone wall

5. Unseen true love of Christopher

6. Rainbow

I am the **beautiful young woman** in the dream. I am wearing a very feminine, soft, flowing dress, which drapes against my body. It is a pale color, off-white, I think, showing my perfect curves, my youthful loveliness. I am fair and my hair is blond, swept up in soft curls. I am feeling completely giving and loving, a saint, ready to give up my life so that the man I love can have his true love who is someone else. I do not hesitate to do this. I have no ulterior motive, no thought of personal gain. I give this freely and with a quiet, serene joy. As I tell him, I see gratitude and love in his eyes and I feel certain of the correctness of my decision.

I am **Christopher Reeve.** I used to play Superman, but now I'm a quadriplegic. Still, I have not lost my joy in living. In this movie, filmed before I was rendered paralyzed in the horse accident, I have my full abilities. The character in this movie is Julie, who is happily sacrificing herself so that I might have my true love. I am grateful, deeply grateful for this opportunity. My love for this other woman is complete and I cannot be fulfilled otherwise. She and I are one and must be together for us to fulfill our destinies. This is important and Julie's sacrifice makes it possible. My life has been one of extremes: Superman to paralysis and helplessness. But in this role, I am on a straight path to my fulfillment.

I am the **Christian icon**. My appearance is at the moment preceding transition. I am ancient, hand-carved wood, carefully painted in rainbows, gold-leafed over the colors, worn a bit by time and touch. I am something you might see in a museum. I have power and prophecy. I am not a *thing*. I have the supernatural power to pass through walls. I am not of this world though I was made in this world. I am much more than what I seem to be. This moment is one of many where I make this change and so does Julie. My presence makes it possible for her to disappear. This is the time.

I am a **stone wall**. My surface is hard and rough, but I am no obstacle for those who are of spirit, those with unselfish love. I am no obstacle though I appear to be an obstacle. I am illusion when one sees beyond form. When clear of mind, when clear of soul, when a choice is made without any doubt, nothing is an obstacle, not even a stone wall.

I am the **true love**. Through me, Christopher will be all he is meant to be, unhampered by obstacles, not even stopped by what he thinks is a paralysis. We are all paralyzed if we allow ourselves to be.

I am the **rainbow**. I come after the rain. There is a pot of gold at the end of me. I am a symbol of hope, of promise, of a future. I am beautiful, colorful, encompassing all colors, blended one into the other harmoniously. When the storm is over, the rainbow comes. I am a smile upside-down. I am the symbol of celebrating diversity, of sexual freedom to be whatever we are.

The dreamer reported feeling very clear and calm after doing this exercise. She was impressed by the voice and tone of the various dream elements and she knew they were speaking to her on a very deep level.

She said, "What I am hearing is that my spiritual life must flower in order for me to transcend the obstacles I thought were in my way. The passive, feminine woman who would give up her life for a man must die in order for me to be all that I can be: powerful, with male energy, and yet still pure of heart. I believe my true love is the work I'm doing today."

I asked her to sum up the messages of the dream, and she said, "All obstacles are illusion. Even a stone wall is permeable with the right spirit. Through the right kind of love and a clear mission, I can be all that I am meant to be. The passive, sweet young woman in me needs to die so I can be Superman." She laughed. "Is this grandiose? Is this right? Something feels correct here though I don't feel like I've fully expressed it properly. If I take into account that I had the dream on the last night of an important retreat, I hear other layers of meaning. I got very clear on what I need in my life that I'm not getting enough of: more time for solitude, quiet, and spiritual growth, time to work on my book with a focus and making it a priority that I haven't done before. This seems very clear to me and I know what I have to do. And another thing occurs to me now. I was very upset at the end of the dream that this woman could disappear without a trace. I think this has to do with my thoughts about my own mortality, that I don't have children. So I feel it's important for me to do something that leaves a lasting impression on the planet. A book is part of that and the time is now."

Wendy did a lot of work on this dream. With hindsight, she was able to say this was definitely a pivotal dream. The images were so different from her usual dreams. "I don't usually dream of famous people, dungeons, or religious icons." She felt that every aspect of the dream seemed to have mythic proportions.

This is certainly a dream that the dreamer can return to and examine again and again for new insight and information. As she put it recently, "Even now, years after this dream, I believe there are messages I have not yet fully grasped. I believe some of these have to do with my spiritual evolution as well as my relationships with men. I also believe this dream told me something about obstacles and how I perceive them. I construct my obstacles. That's a message I need to be reminded of *often!*"

---

NOT long ago, there was a death in my family and I flew to New York for the funeral and to see family members. I had not seen many of these family members since my father's and mother's funerals eleven and ten years before. Living so far from family members and having established such a different life from them, I had some anxiety about returning. Like many people, I had some concern that I would slip back into the old patterns of behavior when I was insecure and needing approval from those who didn't share my values.

In my earlier book, I spoke of having a recurrent dream of being back working in a hospital laboratory, even many years after quitting that job. This metaphor was one I employed frequently in dreams to express feeling unappreciated, overworked, stressed out, and misunderstood. After writing about it in *Dreaming Your Real Self,* I didn't have the dream for several years—until I returned home to Florida from this trip to New York.

## I Don't Need This Job

*I have taken a job again at the hospital where I used to work. This is part-time and I'm doing microbiology again. It's my first day and I have been given pages and pages of forms to fill out and then I am in a long and required conversation with someone. I haven't done any of the microbiology work and the morning is nearly over. Then, a woman I'm supposed to work with comes in upset that I let the coffee run out. She says I should have made more. I say I would have, but I wasn't even in that room the whole morning and didn't have any coffee myself. She is so upset with this that she's going to report me. I know it's ridiculous. Also, another microbiologist hasn't come to work, so they are short-staffed and want me to stay late. I say that I have a client at 12:30 today [which I did have in waking life] and I say I cannot stay late. I am clear that I won't stay no matter what they say. I know that I didn't get my work done because they gave me other things to do. They threaten me with writing me up and bring in a woman who is somebody big in the administration. I can see the pad of pink slips in her pocket, but I'm getting ready to quit myself. I turn to a woman next to me to speak. [She seems like a friend I can say anything to, rather than someone associated with the hospital.] I say to her, "I'm way beyond all this. I have private clients [meaning, therapy work pays better]. I don't need the money here and I'm going to quit before they fire me." The whole thing seems so petty and such low-level stuff that I don't have any patience for it.*

*The woman who comes to give me a formal warning is named Suni. I know she has worked at the hospital for a long time, and I recall [in the dream] that she was there when I worked there before [more than twelve years ago, but no one I can think of in waking consciousness fits this persona]. She thinks she's intimidating with her height (she's VERY tall) and her power, but I think this whole thing is totally dumb and I don't plan to be part of it.*

*The dream ends with me knowing that I'm going to leave. I don't feel afraid or angry—more surprised and detached from the stupid rules they use to persecute people.*

What stands out in this dream is my lack of being upset at any threat that the supervisor will criticize me, write me up, or fire me. I don't care whether they fire me. I am very aware that none of these people has any power over me. I know their judgments are illogical and any evaluation of me is based on not knowing me at all. Significantly, I don't need this job as I once did.

For me, the connection between this dream and a funeral in New York is my feeling before the trip that I would be assessed and judged—perhaps harshly—by my family. This is the equivalent of being written up in my dream. In New York, I heard a lot of their criticism of others whom my family members hadn't seen in many years: "She looks like shit," and "Prepare yourself. She blew up [got fat]." So much of the commentary was about appearance and material possessions that I really didn't want to be part of it at all.

Before the trip, I had decided I'd go as myself whether they liked it or not. I wore my usual uniform: sneakers and socks, tie-dye T-shirt, matching leggings, and no makeup. It was winter in New York and I'm used to Fort Lauderdale's climate. The mental stress was enough and I wanted to be as physically comfortable as possible—one of the ways I take care of myself. I didn't want to buy into their preoccupation with appearance and expensive clothing. The dream supports this detachment.

For me, the message of the dream says that I could go back to an old situation that had once proved to be uncomfortable and I could not be caught up in it this time. It has nothing to do with me. "I'm way beyond this," as I say in the dream.

Granted, the dream statement reveals my *criticism of my family for their values.* (I didn't say I had it all together.) Ideally, the dream would say they could be who they want to be and I could be me and neither of us need feel judged or criticized or in fear of "being fired"—that is, in fear of being rejected or abandoned. But the dream makes the correlation with the old job I left. With many years of hindsight, I can certainly say that quitting was a good decision at the time, though I had my doubts then. The dream says there are parallels with my family—including that the family dynamics are a setup that allows no way to please everyone. In the dream, they give me something to do and then complain that I don't do something else. This is a sort of trap, a no-win situation. Families often play that game, too.

On another layer, this dream is about how I set myself up for being self-critical. No matter what I'm doing, I feel as if I should be doing something else and I beat myself up for not doing the other thing.

When I'm writing, I feel as if I should be reading. When I'm reading, I am sure I should be writing. If I'm doing household chores or cooking, I feel I should be working. I have had to train myself to make a list at the end of the day of all the things I *did* accomplish that day instead of all the things I didn't get done. This dream is also about how hard I am on myself—how unreasonable, how I overwork myself. It says I'm treating myself as I was once treated by others at the hospital. I may be self-employed, but I'm a tough boss. The dream reminds me that this is crazy—that I'm beyond this kind of reasoning (or should be).

Pivotal dreams may be subtle, as my dream suggests. Surely, there are more meanings in this dream than I have room to explore here. But the return of this old dream, especially since it was once a recurrent dream, highlights a real change in my perception of my family and my place among them.

———————

RACHEL dreamed she was in a restaurant with her husband. They have ordered an expensive bottle of wine and an elaborate meal. When the bill arrives, she realizes she has no money and no credit cards with her. They decide to offer the waiter something of value as collateral until they can get money to pay. Rachel reaches inside her purse and pulls out an assortment of household items, starting with a potted plant. Her husband offers music CDs and books from his pockets. They keep pulling out possible offerings, but nothing is worth what their bill costs. Then Rachel pulls out a cuckoo clock, and the waiter says no. This is a moment of high anxiety and the dream ends.

As soon as she woke up, Rachel recognized this as a pivotal dream. She had been consciously concerned about their growing credit card debt and how they would pay it. Rachel managed the money, and she felt that the responsibility for getting control of their spending was up to her. The cuckoo clock said it all—with the humor so common to dreams. For her, this dream provided the threshold for change. Within the week, Rachel and her husband cut up all their credit cards and set themselves on a course to be out of debt within two years—by the turn of the millennium. As they approach that deadline, Rachel is confident they will reach their goal.

---

JANINE had a recurrent dream of remarrying her ex-husband. In her dream, she is marrying him for a third time, even though she is aware in the dream that she really doesn't want to. In waking life, she had been married only once and had been divorced several years. "Do you want to remarry your ex-husband?" I asked, looking at the literal layer first. "No. Even in the dream I don't want to do it." Janine's answer was very congruent—that is, she frowned and shook her head. Her tone, voice, body language, and emotions matched her words.

"What are you married to?" I asked. "What are you married to that you don't want to be married to?" I repeated, using the same metaphor before trying other questions.

Janine smiled and her face flushed deeply. I knew immediately that *she* knew the answer to my question, although I could only guess what it might be. She had had an insight that showed in her body. She might have felt married to her children, a friend, her house or boat, her career, or the Internet. "My job," she said. "It's my job. I work too many hours and then I can't get away from my worries about my job even when I have time off from work."

During the group's self-introductions, Janine had said that she had insomnia and hoped I had some suggestions for her. She said she often lay awake at night thinking about all her worries. Like all dreams, these details make sense in context.

In dreams, we choose the specifics of plot and character to best express what we need to know. Janine was married to her job in that she took it to bed with her every night. Perhaps closer examination would have revealed parallels between the job and her relationship with her ex-husband—how they both seemed to control her time or devour her life, or how the issues that led to divorce seemed without solutions, just as they do at work.

This was a significant dream for Janine. She was able to see how the unraveling of her marriage and the chronic problems in her job had similarities. She could then take this information into action by looking for her own repeating patterns of behavior in two circumstances that might seem, on the surface, to be unrelated. She was free to explore other strategies to address her current difficulties.

———————

ANOTHER woman said she dreamed of a man she thought of as a friend, as well as an occasional sexual partner. When he showed up in her dream as a Nazi and then later as an agent for the secret police, wearing military clothing, she knew she was telling herself this relationship wasn't good for her. "He was very controlling," she said. The dream clarified her feelings and ended her ambivalence about ending the relationship.

———————

EACH of these dreams illustrates the pivotal nature of a strong dream. The strong emotions, bizarre imagery, or haunting atmosphere of the dream draws the dreamer into a deeper level of self-examination. The elements in the dream urge the dreamer farther along his or her life path. The pivotal dream says it is time for a change, time for new action, or time to see the current circumstances in an entirely new way. The pivotal dream says, DO IT NOW!

## DREAMS INTO ACTION

1. Choose one of your dreams that you suspect is pivotal or one that has lingered in your mind for some time.

2. As the dreamer did for *Sacrifice and Disappearance for Christopher Reeve*, list the elements of your dream and speak for each of them. You might want to tape-record this and then tran-

scribe what you say. You will notice changes in your voice and speech pattern that might be clues to other layers of meaning.

3. What new information is contained in this dream?

4. In what way might this dream be pivotal for you at the time of the dream? Now?

5. What might be your first step for taking this dream into life action?

6. What are the possible consequences?

7. What stops you?

8. What makes you eager to take action?

9. What are your thoughts on the elements of the dream *Sacrifice and Disappearance for Christopher Reeve*? What do they mean to you and how might your associations be applicable in your own life?

10. Like Rachel with her cuckoo clock, what metaphor best expresses your financial health? What does your choice of metaphor tell you? How does it point to action?

11. Using the metaphor in Janine's dream, what are you married to that you don't want to be married to? What changes does this suggest to you that you can make now?

12. Using any of the other dreams in this chapter, if it were *your* dream, what would it mean to *you*?

# CHAPTER THREE

# Nightmares

It is in the nature of things to be drawn to the very experiences that will spoil our innocence, transform our lives, and give us necessary complexity and depth.
—Thomas Moore

YOU'VE probably had it happen to you. You wake up in the middle of the night, sweating, out of breath, with your heart pounding. You remind yourself you're safe in bed. It was only a dream. *Another nightmare.* The images are already beginning to fade and you don't really want to remember them anyway. Too scary. Very disgusting. You might wonder if the dream is evidence that you are neurotic. You don't want to think about what it might mean. Likely, you will hesitate to tell anyone about it for fear of their reaction.

Most people have nightmares at some time in their lives. In general, children have more nightmares than adults. Because dreams express how we feel about our lives and what is happening around us on a daily basis, it is not surprising that children's dreams are often frightening. For a child, much of life is confusing and overwhelming, as well as frightening. Everything is big or mysterious. The child lacks the skills and cognitive abilities to make sense of what's happening or to feel as if he or she has any power over what happens. As we get older, we find ways to cope with life and with our worries. As a result, our dream life is also generally less chaotic and terrifying as we grow older. Just as we can handle our problems with more competence in waking life, we seem to handle what our unconscious throws at us in dreams as well.

However, the frequency, intensity, and content of nightmares are highly variable. Some adults have nightmares all their lives and others claim never to have them. Some people have nightmares only when they are living through some crisis or during periods of stress when they feel overwhelmed.

*No matter what you've heard and no matter what the content, having nightmares does not mean you are mentally ill, going crazy, neurotic, violent, abnormal, or evil.* The negative assessment you make about yourself based on a nightmare (or any dream) is likely to be based on not knowing how to understand the way dreams work.

## WHAT IS A NIGHTMARE?

A nightmare is one of many ways our minds try to deal with problems. We usually characterize a dream as a nightmare when the content and emotional impact of the dream leaves us feeling disturbed, frightened, or worried. Nightmares are generally very emotional. They contain themes of physical threat, our own death or the death of someone we know or care deeply about, illness, and the loss of something we value. Emotions in nightmares might be an undercurrent of fear and anxiety—all the way to ultimate terror. We might feel grief, regret, humiliation, guilt, and shame. In the wake of a typical nightmare, both the emotions and imagery of the dream linger, adding to our anxiety—sometimes hours or days later. Until we understand the layers of meaning in the dream, we may remain uneasy and troubled. I have heard people tell a dream they had years ago. As they tell it, the strong uncomfortable feelings of the dream return in the telling. They remain disquieted by the dream until they hear the possible metaphoric meanings and experience the relief that comes with understanding the dream's message beyond its grisly images.

Typical nightmares may be of falls, rape, murder, or mutilating injury through attack. Life-threatening events may come from accidents. What may make the dream "nightmarish" may be the fear of harm by other people (monsters, animals, alien beings). In some cases, the threat is more external than the dreamer's daily interaction with people and places. If the event in the nightmare happened in waking life, we would categorize it as a disaster or tragedy. These catastrophes may be natural, such as hurricanes, tornadoes, tidal waves, floods, and meteors, or they may be human-made disasters such as bombings, war, terrorism, fires, or crashes (planes, cars, trucks, boats, trains). You might say that all nightmares deal with our mortality on some level—overtly or subtly.

The dream may also deal with our emotional fragility—our internal reactions and perceptions. We may be concerned about making fools of ourselves, about being flawed or inadequate in some way.

On many occasions, I have heard someone tell a dream with great feeling and all its repulsive content, without labeling it with the negative term *nightmare*. One woman told of holding a baby in her arms. As she holds this infant, it grows horns, long teeth, and hooves. The baby's face turns bright red. She said it looked like a devil.

I asked, "When did you have this nightmare?"

"It wasn't a nightmare," she answered. "I wasn't scared. I just wondered what was happening."

"Your feeling toward the baby was . . . ?"

"I was curious. Puzzled," she said without hesitation.

I would be inclined to label this dream as a nightmare if I had experienced it, but the dreamer's emotional reaction was more one of wonder and interest. This is a reminder that the dreamer's reaction is the only one that is relevant to the interpretation of a dream.

*When is a dream a nightmare? Only the dreamer can say.*

---

NIGHTMARES are usually unpleasant—most often extremely so. We don't like having them and we don't like the thoughts, feelings, and images that haunt us afterward. We may wish we wouldn't have night-mares at all. If we have them regularly, we wish they would simply stop!

Most of us have had a recurrent nightmare or an unpleasant recurrent dream theme that surfaces periodically like the proverbial bad penny. For others, nightmares are frequent and troubling, making dreamers fearful of their own beds and wishing for a reprieve. Telling someone you're having recurrent nightmares can feel—to some people—like an admission that your mind is out of control. We don't want to be told we're weird—or worse, be given what is often an incorrect diagnosis of our mental condition. At the very least, nightmares are embarrassing. For these reasons, people are frequently afraid to do dreamwork, afraid of what the dream might reveal about them—to others and to them-selves. They don't want to know about their "dark" side.

However, once you understand that dreams come from the part of you that is wiser and more sensible than you usually are, you will welcome dreams, even those that seem terrifying and horrible. A closer look at their messages shows their value. Any nightmare may be a first step to dream back your life. I would say that all nightmares can be approached as pivotal dreams, while not every pivotal dream is a night-mare. For example, my dream of my impending execution sounds like a nightmare to most listeners, but it didn't feel like a nightmare to me—although it turned out to be a pivotal dream. My focus in the dream was on what I had to do, how I needed to spend my time, rather than any fear about death. The dream had more *thoughts and plans* about what to do with my remaining hours than *emotions* such as terror or anger about dying.

A nightmare is one way the unconscious grabs our attention and thrusts important information into our conscious mind. Nightmares contain messages we need to know *now.* The strong emotions solidify the memory of the dream, which is why we are more likely to remember nightmares than pleasant dreams.

Coming from the core of our psyche, where we find our wisest self, the dream makes a statement about our life and our behavior, including our waking perceptions. Often, it offers a new perspective. We create these realistic and outrageous images and set them in a drama to upset our own equilibrium. It is as if the dream grabs us by the shoulders, gives us a good shake, and then shouts, "Listen here! You have to do something now!" The characters and weird events of the dream might cause us to have the feeling of urgency that is often manifested first by our pressing desire to tell the dream to someone—usually a particular someone. Paradoxically we want to tell the dream even as we hesitate because of our embarrassment. *We design our nightmares to catch our full attention so that we will be propelled into action to take back our lives in the way the dream suggests.*

## MYTHS ABOUT NIGHTMARES

Unfortunately, common myths about dreams often stand in the way of acknowledging them as the gifts that they are. Many people still hold the mistaken belief that dreams predict the future or that they are always concrete and literal warnings. Looking into the future for what the dream is predicting will cause you to miss the often profound statement the dream is making about your present problems and how you deal with them.

We have many, many dreams. At five or six dreams each night, we can have more than two thousand dreams a year. Obviously, there is a statistical likelihood that some of those dreams will have content that will correspond with life events after the dream. That doesn't necessarily mean the dream was a prophecy of the future. In fact, we are more likely to remember a dream or nightmare when an event triggers the memory of one. These dreams stand out in the kaleidoscope of dreams. We remember the hits—when the dream matches some aspect of waking reality after the dream—and we forget the misses. The dreams that seem to have no correspondence with waking reality usually fade quickly from our memories.

Because we dream about what concerns us at the time of the dream, dreams contain the choices of action and their many possible outcomes. As in waking thoughts and fantasies, we mull over possible strategies and plans and then evaluate their consequences. When we persist in behaviors that threaten our physical well-being, the health of our relationships, or our economic security, we dream of the negative consequences these actions might create. It is as if, at some deeper level of self-awareness and good sense than we have access to in waking consciousness, we know how we are being self-destructive. In our dreams, we warn ourselves to shape up. In a literal message or in metaphor, the dream might say, "If you continue to smoke, you're going to get lung cancer" (a common dream theme of heavy smokers). Or, "Your high-fat diet is going to give you a heart attack." We know what we need to do to clean up our acts and we nag ourselves in our sleep, just as we do when we're awake.

If my grandmother is ill, I may dream of her dying. If she then dies, this is simply an example of my mind working on a likely outcome of a real situation. There is nothing mystical or magical here. When you ask dreamers what they think their dreams mean, they frequently know this first layer of meaning. "I dreamed that because I was worried about my grandmother."

These dream messages are simply the concerned, rational considerations of our minds. Our intellect has evolved to recognize patterns because this ability has survival value. When we know a pattern, we can be alert to danger and take appropriate action. We learn what's safe and unsafe and change our behavior accordingly to be more effective and efficient. But just as often, we see patterns where, on closer examination, none exist, such as faces on Mars or the moon. We make erroneous connections as we try to make meaning, sometimes generalizing from the particular to the general—a tendency at the root of prejudice and bias of all kinds.

Many people have told me of dreams of a family member having a car crash or being in a plane crash. In their anxiety, they asked the person to delay a trip. In most of these stories, the feared disasters didn't come to pass. The dream often reflected a fear of losing this person at a metaphorical level. A parent may experience the loss of a child as a death when an adult daughter moves away from home to have her own life in another part of the country.

Ironically, this flaw in our critical thinking—overreacting—is often the subject matter that dreams address. By highlighting our fears and projections, dreams force us to look at our reactivity and question our judgment. Here is where the nightmare can be viewed as a gift. Rather than leaping to our usual constructions of reality, an intense dream stops us in our tracks and causes us to ask ourselves questions such as the following:

"Does this make sense?"

"Could this really happen to me?"

"Do I have all the facts?"

"Am I operating out of old childish habits that no longer serve me?"

"Am I making too big a deal of this problem?"

Additionally, we dream about what concerns us and we know where our behavior will lead us if we don't make a change. We know that tension and fighting in a relationship often lead to a separation, that poor work habits lead to getting fired or being the first one chosen for the layoff.

If we look at a disastrous event in a dream as a prediction of a literal incident, we miss the metaphorical message we are telling ourselves that we may be on a *crash course* or *heading for a fall*. We will miss the layers of meaning this particular image that *we personally composed* might convey about all of the different aspects of our lives—career, love, family, creativity. We get stuck in the literal layer and distracted from the real value of the nightmare.

By listening to dreams as predictions of the future instead of metaphors of the present, we miss the thoughtful messages and new viewpoints we offer ourselves.

## CAUSES OF NIGHTMARES

Nightmares are usually caused by the intersection of two conditions:

1. An event in our lives *at the time of the dream,* but immediately preceding the dream, and

2. Our interpretation of that event, often as some physical or psychological threat.

This is true even when the nightmare seems to be a replay of a life event, trauma, or fear that occurred years before the dream. The people and places in the dream may be removed from the dreamer's life for decades, but we still dream about them because they capture a certain constellation of emotions and concerns that are replaying themselves in the present. If I dream I'm back in my childhood home, having an argument with my mother or father, and feeling neglected or rejected as I often did in my childhood, then I ask myself, what is happening in my life now, on the day preceding this dream, that brings up those old emotions of neglect and rejection? How am I feeling rejected now? Who is doing the rejecting? Is this assessment of a person (lover, colleague, friend) accurate? In the words of Gay and Kathlyn Hendricks in *Conscious Loving,* "How am I allowing my past to color my present?"

*A nightmare is a call to action.* It means something is happening in my life that needs a change. An action may be only changing the way I view my circumstance (how I interpret the event) or I may need to do something. Changes in action might be any of a variety of assertive behaviors such as speaking your truth, asking someone else to change the way he or she deals with you, or saying no to something you don't want to do. Other actions may include apologizing for something you did. The dream may assist you in softening your harsh assessment of another person after a disagreement.

In some cases, the dream may be preparing you for more dramatic action such as having a child, going back to school, starting a creative project such as writing a book, initiating the start of a relationship, or ending one.

Other causes of nightmares include chemical changes in the body due to medication, illegal drugs, diet, and exercise. But the content and meanings are useful regardless of what precipitates the nightmare.

## UNDERSTANDING THE VALUE OF NIGHTMARES

When you wake up with your heart pounding, in a sweat of anxiety and real terror, it is hard to step outside these emotions and the horror of the dream to say, "How lovely! This revolting dream is an important gift! How is this a wonderful metaphor about my life? What wisdom is contained here?" While it is sometimes hard to do, approaching a nightmare with the expectation that you will find important and helpful information will immediately change your attitude toward the dream.

While caught in the literal imagery of the dream and the emotions that it creates, it is difficult to hear the metaphor. Several years ago, I had a few dates with a man. Each night, after our date, I had a nightmare. Probably, that should have been enough for me to take action! However, the dreams were in a series—each one indicating what I assessed could go wrong in a possible relationship with this man. This was the last nightmare of the series:

*I am trying to kill my small black poodle. I am squeezing her head, knowing I have to kill her, but simultaneously appalled at what I am doing. I feel this is something I have to do. In the dream, I think, I'm*

*just like Susan Smith, who drowned her two little boys in a car. In this*
*nightmare, I'm aware of this event in the news and it captures my feeling*
*about my behavior. I must be a heartless murderer to kill my own dog.*

I woke up crying and very upset. Of course, I looked immediately
for my two small poodles to be sure they were fine. They were on my
bed, sleeping and safe. I had to remind myself that this was not about
my dog or killing my dog. I forced myself to get my brain in gear and
step out of the feeling of horror at my squeezing my dog's little head
to kill her. I know I would never do that. Where's the metaphor? I
asked.

From working with my dreams on a regular basis, I know that my
dogs represent different aspects of my personality. My small black dog
represents the independent, fearless, adventurous part of me, a part that
I've been nurturing for many years by doing things I fear, including
traveling alone. Coming on the heels of several nightmares that were
more directly connected to the man I had been out with on the evenings
preceding the dreams, I knew this was further commentary on this
developing relationship. What I interpreted the dream to mean was
that to be in a relationship with this man, I had to kill off the independent, fearless, and adventurous part of me. That would be the equivalent to murdering a part of myself, or a developing part of myself. In
that sense, I was being a murderer just like Susan Smith. The compar-
ison was apt and it was a warning to me that this relationship would
be destructive.

You may hear other layers of meaning in this dream, but this is what
seemed *most immediately in the foreground* and required action. A single
nightmare may not be sufficient to spur you to action. But from what
I knew of my interactions with this man, his behavior during a date
preceding the dream, and the whole series of dreams, continuing in the
relationship would be a mistake. It all fit. I didn't see him again.

How do you know when taking action based on the message from
your nightmares is appropriate and not an overreaction? I suggest that
the more dramatic the action is, such as a divorce, changing jobs, or

moving, the more you need to look at a series of dreams. In addition, all decisions should be made as much as possible with conscious intention—that is, using your waking rational mind, setting aside any strong emotions, examining the consequences and choices, and being aware of any motivation that comes out of past wounds or a tendency toward impulsive behavior.

The question of acting on a dream message will be discussed again as we examine individual dreams and the decisions and actions dreamers took based on their meanings.

## VIOLENT DREAMS

If you have violent dreams, it doesn't necessarily mean you are physically violent. People sometimes think dreams reveal their dark side in a way that's completely unknown and foreign to them—as if you could discover you're a murderer from a dream and not have known before that you were capable of murder. Violent dreams, such as mine with my dog, are usually about metaphorical murder or soul murder, as some might prefer to phrase it. If you are doing something violent in a dream, ask yourself what that might represent in your life. What am I killing? What or who am I beating up? If there is a shooting in the dream, how is this a metaphor in my life? Am I taking shots at someone? Who is taking shots at me? Am I shooting myself (in the foot)? Of course, the insults I feel are being inflicted upon me may be the same ones I inflict on someone else. We all have people in our lives who have been overly critical of us, perhaps even discouraging our progress. But the question we must always ask is, How do I do this to others? My mate, children, relatives, friends, and colleagues? The violence in the dream is more often about psychological violence we receive and perpetuate than about literal physical violence.

If, however, you are in a physically abusive relationship with anyone, as the recipient or perpetrator of abuse, seek professional help. You don't have to tolerate abuse. It's a crime.

## SPECIAL SIGNIFICANCE OF NIGHTMARES

Labeling a dream a nightmare indicates you have already concluded that it holds a special significance to you. Whatever happened in this dream left you with strong emotions. Perhaps the dream woke you or was extremely vivid. Nightmares that are especially weird or bizarre are shouting at you, too, reminding you that the issue the nightmare addresses can no longer be ignored. These are all signs that the dream message is more important than those of dreams that fade quickly when you get up or those that can't be recalled no matter how hard you try. Nightmares are special. On some level, we know they are special, which accounts for our desire to tell the dream to someone else and why we mull it over. When the dream lingers, as nightmares often do (by definition), we are acknowledging their special significance. Even our *not* wanting to tell our nightmares highlights their special nature. Getting past this fear and telling the dream to a trusted friend or dream partner will help you see how the nightmare is a gift.

## RECURRENT NIGHTMARES

When you have recurrent nightmares, then you are trying to tell yourself something and you are not listening to the message. Something is troubling you, but you are not addressing the problem.

On some level, you already know what the problem is, which is why you have told yourself this dream. It could be anything in your life, such as an ongoing problem with a close friend, a conflict at your job, feeling dominated or oppressed by someone in your life, health issues, or a psychological or emotional concern in the past or present that you haven't yet dealt with. The nightmares will likely continue until you address the problem. That might mean getting professional help to develop some skills to deal with the problem, such as learning to speak your truth (be more assertive) or giving yourself permission to develop your own talents and abilities and to find satisfying work.

When I speak to public audiences, people will often say they had a recurrent nightmare for many years, but they no longer have this dream. "When did it stop?" I ask. They think a moment and then laugh because they stopped having the nightmare after some major change in their lives. Commonly, they no longer had the dream after they moved out of their parents' home, married, divorced, moved, or changed jobs or careers. While they didn't connect the nightmare with these events in their lives, they solved the problem by changing their life circumstances and the dream stopped. Had they consciously addressed the problem in the years while they were having the nightmare, the nightmares would have stopped sooner. They might also have solved their problems soon enough to avoid a divorce or illness.

One woman told of a recurrent nightmare of being lost in a public place. She said the dream varied. Sometimes she was on unfamiliar city streets, sometimes in a rural setting. At other times, she couldn't find her car or she was using public transportation and had taken the wrong bus. The overwhelming sense of being lost was a recurrent theme of these nightmares.

I asked her in what way she felt she was lost in her daily life. She looked down and held back tears. "I am lost. I'm sixty-seven years old and I still don't feel as if I've really lived my own life. I've been taking care of everyone else and not thought about what I wanted. Now my husband is dead and my children are grown and moved away to the four corners of the country. And I'm lost."

This woman is like many in her age group who have raised families and neglected their own needs and personal development. For men, the insight is often that they have ignored their loved ones in the service of their careers. They may suddenly discover in their fifties that they want to enjoy the pleasures of family and connection.

The discussion of her recurrent nightmare was a turning point for this woman. It highlighted what she already knew. She was able to take action and pursue a childhood desire to be an artist.

## REMEDIES FOR RECURRENT NIGHTMARES

Your nightmares probably have some pattern to them. Notice when the recurrent dream started, when you have it, and if it stopped, when that was. What does this pattern tell you? Do you always have the dream after spending time in a certain place or in the company of certain people? How does this dream capture a certain group of emotions? Your choice of metaphor (being chased rather than being smothered, for instance) comes from your own use of metaphor in your everyday speech. How do you talk about feeling tired, overwhelmed, or burdened in your daily life? When you address these issues, the nightmare will stop. Keeping a journal on a regular basis helps you see these patterns of dreaming and problems and how they mirror one another.

---

NATALIE dreamed of escaping from a dangerous building.

> I escape from a collapsing building. Outside, I'm safe, but I realize I have to go back into the building to get some important papers. I know it's dangerous, but I go back. I decide I'll go only to the third floor.

This dream was discussed in a private dream group where the members knew each other. To the dismay and concern of her friends, Natalie had recently announced her decision to reconnect with her ex-boyfriend. Her friends worried because they knew Natalie had been unhappy in the relationship and so far had had a hard time getting away from him. Natalie's dream seemed to be a warning that her relationship was a collapsing building—dangerous to reenter. What did the important papers she needed in the dream symbolize? What did going only to the third floor mean? Natalie's friends came on strong, *telling* her the dream was conclusive evidence of the error she was making. Predictably, Natalie resisted their interpretation because she hadn't arrived at it herself. She acted as if she didn't understand the meaning of the dream at all and didn't offer any interpretations of her own.

Months later, after Natalie had reunited with her ex-boyfriend, it was clear *to her friends* that she wanted this relationship because of the financial security she believed it would offer—symbolized by the important papers. Going only to the third floor might have suggested her limited commitment to the relationship or her plan to stay only long enough to get the financial security she came for. But that was the assessment of those who knew her. Natalie didn't confirm this interpretation.

---

ANOTHER dreamer, Jesse, told a dream of hearing an old song that reminded him of a former lover. In the dream, Jesse is with his current lover, Bill, and is embarrassed by his strong reaction to this old song. He steps out of the room to weep in privacy. When he steps outside, he is in a beautiful garden. Suddenly there is a filament of wire at his neck. He attempts to break it and discovers it's a spider web and he cannot break it loose. A short distance away, he sees a huge spider coming closer and closer to him.

This dream opened up several areas of exploration for Jesse. He compared his present relationship with those in his past, including the one in the dream. The term *web* brought many associations that bore fruitful discussion. For Jesse, it meant the World Wide Web, where he did Web site design—a new career for him and one that was going well. He discussed his web of relationships and how they affected one another—sometimes unfavorably. He felt he was still caught in the web of a past relationship that threatened his current, healthy one.

Jesse also brought up the idea of a web of lies. He remembered the first time he had been caught in a lie and how that experience had been pivotal in his life. In telling a false story, he had created a flurry of attention around himself that had, for a long time, encouraged him to continue to weave his web of lies. He saw how destructive that could be, symbolized by the spider and its web to snare unsuspecting prey.

After exploring the various avenues the dream pointed toward, Jesse could then see the nightmare as the gift it was. Jesse took some steps to deal differently with the former lover who might have sabotaged his current relationship if Jesse hadn't intervened. Jesse took the actions he deemed necessary.

## Steps for Conquering Nightmares and Recurrent Dreams

1. When does this nightmare or recurrent dream occur?

2. Any new chemicals or medications? *ALWAYS consult your doctor before making any changes in your prescription medication.*

3. How is this nightmare a *metaphor* of your present life situation?

4. What most concerns you? How is the dream a statement of this concern?

5. What is the dream telling you that you need to know *now*?

6. What do you need to do or change in your life *right now*? The dream will stop when you make this important change.

### CONCLUSION

To stop recurrent nightmares, you must do something different from what you are doing now. *A nightmare is a call to action.* If you've had the dream and remembered it, *you already know,* on some level of your consciousness, what you need to change. How you do that will be an unfolding process, perhaps revealing itself to you over time in many dreams. Some later dreams may appear trivial or silly. They may lack the punch of the very memorable nightmare, but they often contain information that will help you as you make changes to live the kind of life you want.

Each night, in our dreams, we talk to ourselves, telling stories about our own lives and other possible ways to live them. But most of us aren't listening—partly because we were never taught the skills to listen. *A nightmare is a gift in bright lights and weird packaging.*

Important messages come to us in the metaphors of the dream story. Listening to these messages often means that we will experience some discomfort or upheaval in our lives, especially as we take action.

My friend Gale says, "Transformation is never fun while it's happening." I would like to add, "But afterward, we know the struggle was worth it."

## DREAMS INTO ACTION

1. Write out your recurrent nightmare and then read it over. Circle all the words that express the violence or create fear in your dream, such as *drowning, running, shooting, bleeding,* or *dying.*

2. What is like the nightmare in your waking life?

3. What are the emotions in the dream? The different emotions in the nightmare will point to different actions in your life. If you are disgusted or repulsed in the dream, that is very different from feeling your life is threatened by a monster.

4. Without offering your own interpretation first, allow someone else to read your dream and tell you what he or she hears. This works best with someone who knows you well, a person whom you trust and who supports your growth and independence. Alternatively, you can ask someone who doesn't know you at all and try on what he or she has to say. Remember that whatever anyone else, including an "expert," says about your dream

can only be a projection of their own issues onto the metaphors of your dream. You are the true expert on the meaning of your dream. But since so many of us have the same issues to resolve in our lives, someone else's thoughts might help you to step outside your dream and see it in new ways you wouldn't have thought of on your own.

*Caution:* Don't let others tell you that their interpretation is correct. Consider what feels as if it fits for you. Look for your own interpretation.

5. Ask yourself how the elements of the dream were metaphors for your life circumstances *at the time of the dream.*

6. If you were listening to the messages of your nightmares, what would you hear?

7. Based on these messages, what would you *do* if you were fearless and had unlimited resources?

8. Does your answer scare you? Is it too big a change? Do you see too many obstacles?

# CHAPTER FOUR

# Childhood Dreams

What a delight this is! All this inventing, this producing,
takes place in a pleasing, lively dream.
—Wolfgang Amadeus Mozart

MANY people have a childhood dream or remember an old dream even after many years. Dreams that linger frequently remain puzzling or disturbing and continue to make us wonder about their meaning.

When a dreamer tells an old dream, we can look at what it might have been communicating at the time of the dream. But we can also look upon the meanings of the dream in the present—at the time it is remembered and retold. What is this dream communicating at these two points in time? And what might be its larger meaning for the person's life? What is the urgency to tell this dream today? What is its current relevance?

## TECHNIQUES FOR WORKING WITH OLD DREAMS

As with any dream, follow the twenty steps for dreamwork on pages 54–5. Here are additional steps for working with an old dream:

1. Tell the dream in present tense, just as you would with a current, new dream.

2. Give all the details of the dream, even if they appear to be trivial.

3. What were your emotions for each event in the dream?

4. What were your emotions at the end of the dream?

5. What were your emotions on waking from the dream?

6. What is it about this dream that makes it particularly vivid?

7. What was happening in your life at the time of the dream?

8. What was your age then?

9. What concerns did you have at that time?

10. How were these problems resolved?

You now have the benefit of hindsight on your life and on this dream. You know how things turned out or changed in your life. This is the reason why old dreams often seem less mysterious than they do at the time of the dream. They also lose some of their emotional charge over time.

In the light of the historical context that you now have, what do you think this dream was communicating to you at the time of the dream?

At a workshop, a man told a dream that was several years old. Here is his summary of the dream.

> *I am very worried about my baby brother. A woman kidnaps him and attacks him. I can't save him and he is killed. I woke up feeling very worried and afraid for him. It still scares me when I tell it.*

I asked the man what was happening at the time of the dream. Though he thought of the dream as "old," he remembered the context.

The dreamer's brother had been dating a woman that he, the dreamer, didn't like. In fact, the woman had later threatened his brother with a charge of rape and they had broken up.

"Okay. That tells me this was a dream about a real, literal concern in your life at the time of the dream. That's layer one. To go deeper, what did this dream have to do with you at the time of the dream?"

At first, the dreamer didn't think it had anything to do with him. I asked, "Is there any parallel, literally or metaphorically, between your brother's situation and your own?"

He was quiet for a few moments as all of us waited to see if he made any connection. "I was dating someone then. . . . She was really a nice girl. . . ."

His voice and tone said otherwise, so I asked further, "Was she?"

He laughed nervously and said quickly, "She did stalk me after we broke up."

"The nice girl stalked you?"

"I guess I was worried about my own safety, too."

"Good. That's layer two—at the time of the dream. But you could have chosen any dream to tell today to get our help and clarity. Because you picked this old dream to tell, I'm wondering what significance it holds for you right now."

The man blushed, the muscles of his face lost their earlier tension, and his frown disappeared. His mouth opened in an O. From these changes in his expression, we all knew he was having a big *aha*. He knew exactly what the significance was and we all had our educated guesses. Then he suddenly laughed aloud and covered his face with his hands, typical signs that he had made a real connection—an insight.

"You don't have to tell us. We know that you know and that's all that counts. You don't have to share it. You know what it's about today?" I asked.

He nodded and gestured to the back of the room. "My friend back there is jumping out of her seat."

"Then you probably know what to do, too," I added.

THIS dream may sound more like an unsolved mystery than a big insight. Because I wanted to respect the man's privacy—especially in public—I didn't press him to give the details of his current situation. It was clear to most of us that he was again in a relationship that was potentially threatening. He knew it and he seemed to need to tell this dream to get it out in the open. Perhaps he needed to hear himself say it and to feel supported in making some change in the current dangerous relationship. I don't know whether the change or action called for by the dream meant breaking off the relationship or being more assertive within the relationship. I have no idea whether these insights were about a romance or a friend. He might have felt threatened by a family member or a colleague at work. The important outcome was that he knew he had to take action—the message of all dreams.

Like most of us, he was repeating a mistake similar to one he had made before, as well as similar to his brother's mistake. This old dream still haunted him because he was caught up in an old pattern that he needed to change.

## RECURRENT CHILDHOOD DREAMS OR NIGHTMARES

If you had a recurrent dream in childhood that you still remember and would like to know what it was about, keep in mind that the dream was about what was going on in your life each time you had it. You created the dream to come to terms in some way with your waking reality. Most children have dreams of being chased by monsters or hiding from them. They dream of disasters, especially of the loss or death of their parents and siblings—those people in their lives that mean support, protection, nurturance (food, warmth, clothing), safety (both physical and psychological), love, and acceptance.

As discussed in the chapter on nightmares, the world is a sometimes scary place for children. Depending on their age, children experience many things as bigger than they are, difficult to understand, and mostly out of their control. They don't have the physical or mental skills to solve problems and deal with the unexpected events that life brings— those abilities that we develop with experience and maturity. Children have a hard time placing the emotions and behaviors of others in context. For example, a child will surely know when there is tension in the family relationships, but might not be able to explain why Dad is so upset and Mom isn't home for dinner. It all simply feels bad to her. Something is dangerously wrong. It may be more confusing if nothing is explained to the child. If adults are trying to shield her from unhappy information or protect her from knowledge that may be disturbing, the uncertainty may raise anxiety. If adults deny the reality of a miscarriage, abortion, financial problems, marital discord, or illness, the child may be aware that something is wrong or feel she is being lied to. Denying the child's perception of events around her may teach her to doubt her own feelings and perceptions. Any of these circumstances may trigger a nightmare for the child. At the same time, children should not be offered information that they are too young to comprehend or handle. It's a delicate balance between honesty and reassurance.

The same kinds of difficult circumstances will cause us nightmares as adults. In our dreams, we attempt to solve problems and resolve the dissonance between opposing views and feelings. If someone tells us everything is fine and we know it isn't, we may feel betrayed by and distrustful of those who try to protect us.

Childhood dreams and nightmares were attempts by your dreaming self *at the time of the dream* to resolve those issues that disturbed you *then*. Follow these twenty steps to work with the childhood dream that still seems a mystery now.

## 20 Steps for Dreamwork

1.  Record the dream in specific detail as soon as possible.

2.  What are the main events of the dream?

3.  What are your dominant feelings during the dream? At the end of the dream? When you wake up? What is the contrast between these waking and dreaming emotions?

4.  Describe each dream element: person, animal, place, or thing.

5.  What do these descriptions remind you of?

6.  What are your feelings related to each description?

7.  What were you thinking about when you went to bed before the dream?

8.  What were the main events of your day?

9.  What happened the day of the dream that left you with feelings similar or in contrast to those of your dream?

10. What do your descriptions from the dream resemble in your life circumstances at the time of the dream?

11. Summarize the dream in one sentence.

12. How is this dream a *metaphor* for your:

    *   Relationships? (friendships, children, lover, spouse, co-workers)
    *   Family of origin and childhood wounds?
    *   Inner self? Mental or emotional state?
    *   Professional or work life?
    *   Spiritual life?
    *   Personal history?
    *   Body's health?
    *   Creative health?
    *   Relationship to the planet or universe?

13. What subpersonalities or unknown aspects of yourself does the dream expose?

14. What new information does this dream bring to light?

15. How is this a more honest statement about your current situation?

16. What action does the dream call for?

17. What other possible meanings does this dream hold?

18. If this were someone else's dream, how would you interpret it? What does the metaphor say to him or her? What questions might you want to ask this dreamer?

19. How do you feel now?

20. Phrase a specific question to ask for another dream.

Further work:

◆ Have dialogues with dream characters and animals.

◆ Draw, paint, or sculpt the dream images and/or feelings.

◆ Dramatize and exaggerate the dream actions and feelings.

◆ Use dream stories and images for creative inspiration.

Also consider the following:

◆ What does the dream seem to be about?

◆ How is the dream a metaphor for your life at the time of the dream?

◆ If the dream was recurrent, can you see a pattern in the timing or frequency of this dream? What does its occurrence correlate with?

Of course, all of these questions are harder to answer when the dream is old rather than current. Our associations today to the dream elements, and therefore their possible meanings, may have no resemblance to what they might have meant at the time of the dream. We may not be able to place the dream in a specific period or we may not remember its context.

However, sometimes having distance from a dream makes it easier to understand its meaning. The emotions are not so raw and striking, and we are not so attached to the literal images. Frequently, we've already resolved the issues the dream was dealing with at the time of the dream. Today, it may refer to something different but similar. With a little help, we can make the connection to possible meanings.

---

MELISSA is a woman in her sixties who told a recurrent childhood dream she'd had when she was about six years old. The dream setting is in her grandmother's home, which she frequently visited. Melissa also spent time with a neighbor's family in an apartment upstairs where there were two boys several years older than she.

> I go up the stairs to the neighbor's apartment and the landing is very dark—as it really was. As I get to the landing, I disappear into a hole. Nothing there. I just fall through and disappear. A scary dream.

As we talked about this dream, Melissa recalled seeing this family in later years when she was about fourteen. One of the boys made repeated sexual advances that she had to fend off. Melissa wondered whether her fearful dream was about some earlier attempt by this boy or his brother when they were ten and thirteen. That was possible, even though she had no specific memory of any such event. For a six-year-old, having to be alone in a darkened stairway may be enough to cause anxiety. Perhaps she felt the boys were predatory or aggressive as well, and this triggered the recurrent dream. At the time, she was an only child and her home life was unstable. Her parents were constantly arguing and they moved frequently, leaving her at her grandmother's home. The image and sensation of falling into a hole and disappearing captures a child's anxiety well.

Because the dream was so old yet still carried an emotional charge in the present, I asked the dreamer in what way she feared falling into a hole today. How is *a hole* a metaphor for something in your life now?

Melissa immediately responded by saying that she was worried that she would end up a bag lady. She spoke loudly and quickly, with the energy of conviction. I asked her whether this was a realistic fear. She elaborated that her husband had invested her money and lost most of it. He was unwilling to explain what he'd done and she felt unable to ask for more information. His shady dealings worried her, but she no longer had her own financial resources to support her if he didn't. She seriously worried that she could end up homeless in her old age—or find herself compelled to live with one of her adult children. She said it was a real concern.

Then Melissa added, speaking more softly and almost as an afterthought: "I was very poor as a child. I had only hand-me-downs for clothing. The food at the table was measured out and you couldn't ask for more. I don't want to go back to that."

The old dream images and her current concerns have parallels: The word *shady* may be associated with a darkened stairwell. Having no support today may be the same as falling into a hole in the dream. And her fear of having to stay with her children is like being dumped off at her grandparents' home when she was a child.

Melissa was able to make connections between her current concerns and the meanings of her old recurrent childhood dream.

---

IF you're still stumped by a childhood dream, here are some suggestions for further work:

- Tell your dream to a parent and ask for his or her reaction. Probe gently. You may be on more sensitive territory than you think. If you hesitate to do this, ask yourself what holds you back. This can be a strong clue to the meaning of the dream. You might ask your parent the question in a letter and give him or her time to answer. Or you might imagine the response and write it out in the words he or she would likely use, stepping outside of yourself a little by doing this and letting yourself think in new ways.

- Tell your dream to a sibling and ask for his or her reaction. You can do this whether your sibling is older or younger. The metaphors of your dreams will likely resonate with others who lived in the same household. That is, family members often speak the same language of metaphors, symbols, clichés, expressions, and curses, and may have similar psychological issues that come up in dreams.

- Tell your childhood dream to someone who knows you well. Preferably, this would be some other family member or a friend or mate/lover you've had for more than ten years. These people know more about you and how your mind works than you think they do. They may easily hear something in a dream that escapes your attention. Because they are not bogged down in the literal interpretations, they can more easily hear the metaphor. This is often true of doing dreamwork with others. They will have their own blind spots about their own dreams. This is why group dreamwork is so powerful.

- In each of these possible explorations, be open to what others have to say. Remember that you are always the expert on the meaning of your own dreams. Whatever they say will certainly be colored by their own beliefs about themselves and about you. No one has a monopoly on the truth, especially when it comes to dreams. Each dream holds many truths.

- When asking others for their thoughts about your dream—any dream, old or current—you are not asking them to tell you what your dream means. How could they know, when you made up the dream for yourself? Instead, you are asking for their contribution of another perspective, perhaps one you would never see on your own. But remember, you are always the final expert on the meaning of your dreams and how they can change your life.

## EXAMINING OLD DREAMS FOR TODAY'S GUIDANCE

Once you have some theories about what an old dream meant at the time of the dream, begin to think about what it might mean for you today. I suspect that old dreams still hold a charge when the concerns that triggered the dream are still unresolved or unfinished in some way. Like Melissa, you can look beyond the meaning at the time of the dream for its relevance for your life now.

1. How does this dream address a pattern in my life?

2. In what way is this dream about my core issues? (Recall the discussion of core issues in Chapter 1.)

3. How does this dream connect with my problems today?

4. If this old dream is still calling for a change in my life, something I've neglected taking care of for years, what might that change be?

5. What present circumstances in my life mirror the events and emotions in my life at the time of this old dream?

6. If this dream were someone else's, what would I say it could be about?

## LIMITATIONS TO WORKING WITH
## OLD DREAMS

When doing dreamwork, it's always important to remember that we tell ourselves *this* dream at *this* time because it has current relevance. When doing dreamwork, we ask the dreamer to make associations with the elements of the dream. This and the emotional content of the dream are some of the key pointers to the dream's meaning. With an old dream, we are making today's associations with a dream symbol that we chose at the time of the dream—perhaps years or decades ago. The symbol made very good sense to the dreamer on the day of that dream, which is why he or she chose it. This makes deciphering the symbol today more difficult than when a dream is fresh. Further, the issues that were in the foreground for the dreamer—the concerns that were pressing enough to create a dream—are frequently resolved with time. Unless you can remember the context in which the dream took place— the more detailed the better—it may be difficult to uncover the meanings in an old dream.

## THE VALUE OF WORKING WITH
## OLD DREAMS

When you work on an old dream and you are able to have an insight about it in the present, you have another opportunity to do something about an old issue. With distance from the problem, more experience, and more wisdom, you can do something now that you may have been unable or unwilling to do at the time of the dream. Perhaps you lacked the resources, such as the time, money, energy, and confidence that you have now. You may have lacked the mature understanding and perspective you have now to take the dream into action. You can use the insights from an old dream to take a step to get unstuck in your work or in your relationships or in your most important relationship—the one you have with yourself. The dream can be looked upon as an occasion to reevaluate your priorities—how you spend your time, your money, and your energy. You can take action to shift your focus or begin to accomplish a goal that's been shelved for too long.

The woman who had the recurrent childhood nightmare of the darkened stairwell was reminded of her fear of a return to the poverty of her childhood, this time at an older age. It forced her to look at her financial situation and take a more active role in money management along with her husband.

By working with an old dream, you can get some hints at what you need to do to take back your life. An old dream that haunts you may be like a thorn in your side prodding you to take action.

## DREAMS INTO ACTION

1. List three or more old dreams that you recall.

2. Choose the one with the strongest feelings and most vivid imagery.

3. Write this dream down in detail, including the setting, emotions, events, and dream characters. Note your age in the dream, and pinpoint as accurately as possible when you had the dream.

4. What was happening in your life at the time of the dream?

5. How do those events mirror the dream's emotional tone or the story that the dream tells?

6. Summarize the story in two or three sentences.

7. How does the dream end?

8. What issues does the dream try to resolve at the time you had the dream?

9. If it haunts you now, what statement is it making about parallels between present and past events in your life? (Remember that the man who dreamed about his brother's dangerous relationships was in one of his own.)

10. What action does this dream call for you to do now?

11. Make a journal entry about these insights so that they don't evaporate like unrecorded dreams.

CHAPTER FIVE

# Dream Signposts and Endings

The eye sees a thing more clearly in dreams than the
imagination awake.

—Leonardo da Vinci

## WHAT IS A SIGNPOST?

Signposts include bizarre behavior in the dream, especially an action
that would be completely out of character with the dreamer's or the
dream character's waking personality, or a puzzling image or location
that occurs repeatedly. An animal or figure may appear with a cryptic
phrase or sentence spoken or communicated telepathically to the
dreamer. These symbols stand out because they have a special purpose.
Uncovering their layers of meaning can propel the dreamer into a deeper
level of self-awareness and may open new avenues for living.

Some specific details in dreams stand out from all the others. A
peculiar juxtaposition of dream elements is often a sure sign that the
dream holds a very personal and special meaning. These may be signposts in one dream or those that recur in many dreams. Another signpost can be a particular dream ending.

Sometimes a single piece of evidence can crack a criminal investi-
gation. One piece of the puzzle brings the jumble of parts into a complete picture. Similarly, a dream's ending may provide the piece that

completes the puzzle. In this chapter, we'll look at dream signposts and endings as indicators of how we handle our emotions, solve problems, and interpret our world. By examining these outcomes and how they parallel our waking strategies, we can make a conscious decision to change our behavior to be more in keeping with our life goals. That is, what we do in dreams to handle our dilemmas reveals how we handle our waking problems. By gaining an awareness of a pattern of behavior or thinking, we can make changes. We can take steps to be more authentic and intentional instead of continuing our patterns of playing a role and holding back from life.

For example, if I hide from a problem (symbolized as a monster) or deny it in a dream, perhaps I do the same thing in waking life. With this awareness, I am more willing to face my problems and solve them.

## SIGNPOST CHARACTERISTICS

Signposts are dream elements that are particularly beautiful, grotesque, fantastic, absurd, or recurrent, or carry an emotional charge. They can be images that repeat themselves in many dreams, sometimes to the dismay of the dreamer. They are flags, signals, and beacons, pointing the way to something significant.

An example for Elke was the recurrent image of dirty bathrooms with globs of human feces on the floor. Elke was revolted by all this "shit" and somewhat embarrassed when telling these dreams. In each of these dreams, she feared being blamed for making this mess and having to clean it up. Some of the questions the dream group asked her were the following:

What shit do you keep walking into in your life?

Who is shitting things up?

Who is giving you shit?

Whose shit do you have to clean up? Is it really yours?

If you have to go, what do you want to let out or unload?

If you find yourself disgusted by this dream image, you can imagine how Elke felt when it appeared in her dreams several times in a row. However, the word *shit* was one she used frequently in her everyday language, especially to express her anger at certain aspects of her life. In many ways, Elke felt constrained from expressing her true feelings and her true self at her job and with her family members. She was afraid of being labeled strident when she spoke with passion and gusto. And so she held everything in, but found herself wading in other people's shit—their emotional outpourings—instead.

This symbol was a signpost for Elke. Each time it came up, she could reflect on how she was holding her own emotions in check while letting others express theirs. She would then ask herself what it would mean for her to let her own stuff out and where it might be safe to do that.

———————

MELISSA, whose recurrent childhood dream of falling into a hole was discussed in Chapter 4, noticed a signpost in her dreams. After several weeks of dreamwork, she realized that in nearly every dream, she was changing her clothes, shopping for clothes, choosing accessories, or making note of decor and design in her surroundings. Her dreams had enormous details about what she was wearing and what others were wearing in the dream—more than just a point of plot or an identifier for a character. Melissa's dream group began to expect images of clothing and appearance. We all wondered aloud what she was trying to tell herself with this regular feature of her dream. Without hesitation, Melissa said that she had always wanted to be a fashion designer and had considered ideas on and off over the years about what kinds of clothing and accessories she would design. That desire still called to her. At the same time, she was doing volunteer work with children and she wanted to continue to offer children what she had to give, while simultaneously nourishing her own spiritual growth and theirs.

I suggested Melissa make a list of at least 100 possible professions that might incorporate these aspects of her authentic self (designing, spirituality, working with children) and see what came up on the list. Then I said she could narrow the list down to five to ten things that seemed to bring her talents and desires together best. Because this list is more like brainstorming, no critical analysis or discussion of obstacles here is necessary. (See Kathleen Adams's book *Journal to the Self*.)

Here's Melissa's narrowed-down list of seven professions and her journal entry afterward.

Jewelry designer

Fashion designer

Fabric designer

Spiritual mentor

Greeting card designer

Fabric painter

Children's spiritual book writer (pre-kindergarten to fourteen-year-olds)

It seems obvious to me from my list that creative design is still a big part of my psyche. The spiritual aspect of my development craves expression also, as does my writing, though to a lesser degree.

A short while ago, it dawned on me that all of these dreams about clothing and trying on and shopping and accessories might be my unconscious trying to kick my door in. "Stupid! Wake up! You know what you want to do. You've always known what you want to do. What you have a need to do. You need more help? More direction? Here! Use your spiritual side to meditate on ideas. You have a soft spot for children?

Fine! Think about directing it toward teaching children loving-kindness for themselves and others. But you don't need to devote your efforts exclusively to children."

What is important is touching people's lives in a positive and loving way. It is important that they pass it on to people whom they come in contact with. I certainly like the things that lots of money can buy, but this is not an important goal. Being of service while expressing my need for creativity is foremost.

Melissa also remembered an earlier dream that she had titled *Cape-Abilities*. She said her dreams had even given her the name for her future business. She plans to design lightweight stoles and wraps in a variety of styles and colors, some beaded and appliquéd. Wearable art. Perfect, Melissa says, for air-conditioned buildings and restaurants in South Florida.

"Think big," I whispered.

Melissa is still working on this project.

## TRACKING SIGNPOSTS

To track the signposts in your own dreams, you will need to collect your dreams over a period of time—at least a few months. If you've been keeping a journal that includes your dreams, you probably already have several dreams to use to begin to look for patterns. You may have already observed some pattern in your style of dreaming, such as certain themes that show up repeatedly, a favorite symbol, or a setting or place that you use again and again.

To track your signposts, you can read through your recorded dreams from a particular time, especially intervals of intense dreaming, and mark them with highlighters in different colors or Post-it notes to keep track of patterns. For example, every time you dream of a bear, you could highlight the word *bear* in yellow. If you frequently have dreams of driving or swimming, what commonly happens in the dream? You might make notes in the margin of your dream journal to locate this repeating theme or use Post-it notes or colored flags to mark them.

Now ask yourself the following questions:

1. What symbol frequently shows up in my dreams? We all have favorite symbols that we use regularly. We choose them because they perfectly represent what we are trying to say to ourselves. If you frequently dream of water, what kind of water is it? What is the emotional tone and how does it reflect your own emotions? A hurricane is a very different symbol of water than a calm lake.

2. What animals, if any, are characters in my dreams? Animals may be a kind of signpost. We anthropomorphize animals in our dreams, as we do in waking life, attributing certain human characteristics to them. These traits may be aspects of our own personalities that we have not yet integrated and owned. An example might be bravery or fearlessness. The animal is strong and powerful in ways we would like to be, but don't know we *already are*. The scary animal in your dream may be the powerful part of you!

3. What am I doing in my dreams? What is the relationship between this activity and my waking life and activities? (Remember that Melissa frequently dreamed about shopping for clothes and changing her clothing. You dream about what is important to you.)

4. How do I feel in my dreams? Emotions such as feeling lost or out of place may be signposts that you are on a life quest to find your purpose. What you are searching for in the dream may be a clue to what you need to be searching for in your

waking life. (We'll look at more examples of hints to your life quest in later chapters.)

If you have a dream partner or a dream group that you attend, the people who do dreamwork with you are likely to have noticed patterns in your dream subjects and symbols. You can ask them what they see as a pattern or what they think might be a signpost in your dreams.

———————

ONE man, Richard, had repeating themes of being abducted in his dreams. Sometimes, he seemed to be a small boy again, carried off by an older adult. He said that one person told him this was evidence of having been kidnapped, perhaps by aliens. Richard thought this was ridiculous and came to me because he knew the dream must have some symbolic meaning.

In these dreams, Richard said he still had his waking adult consciousness, but he felt unable to protest or to defend himself in any way. He was also unable to call for help. Richard said he felt as if he couldn't complain or say no to the people who carried him off. He felt powerless.

I repeated these words to him and asked how this reflected some aspect of his life. He had an immediate *aha*. He was brought up to go along with the wishes of others, and was taught not to be difficult or "contrary." Now, as an adult, he often acquiesced to the wishes of others, including those of his supervisor at work and his elderly parents. He had never learned how to say no to a request or to state his own wishes. In a way, he had allowed himself to be abducted by others. This signpost contributed to Richard's ability to decide to learn some basic assertiveness techniques. In this way, he could finally begin to live his own life and sometimes get what *he* wanted, too, even while pleasing others.

———————

IN an ongoing dream group, Jesse, mentioned on page 45, repeatedly had dreams of driving, most often in the town where he grew up. In nearly every dream, he had to turn around and go back to where he came from or he was constantly making U-turns.

The group asked Jesse how this reflected something in his waking life. Although it seemed clear to all of us who had heard his dreams and the principal issues in his life for months, it took a while for Jesse to take action on what he knew and what his dreams kept telling him. He was going back over old ground, continually repeating his old mistakes and allowing his guilt to call him back into an old situation. He knew he needed to let go. He said he needed to *move on down the road and not backtrack.* When he was able to recognize this—in another dream with entirely different symbolism—he felt enormous relief and was surprised he hadn't been able to do it sooner.

Of course, we can only do what we're ready to do and *when* we're ready to do it—no matter how many signposts our unconscious holds up to us. Just knowing what a problem is or what we *should* do is often not enough. We may first need to confront other issues such as our fear or guilt before we can move on.

## DREAM ENDINGS AND OUTCOMES

Dream endings are also signposts. How the problem in a dream is resolved and what the dreamer *does* in the dream to deal with what's happening, particularly in a nightmare, points to how the dreamer copes in waking life. If the dreamer does something in a dream that he thinks he would never do in waking life, that is likely to be a signpost, too. Do you hide from the monster? Do you fight back? Do you keep silent in the face of an accuser? Are you resigned to a situation not being in your control? These may be signposts or clues for dealing with the difficulties of your waking life.

When I said this at a public talk, one woman said that she was always running away in her dreams. Without any prompting, she wondered aloud whether this meant that she usually ran away from her problems rather than facing them. She laughed and added, "That *is* what I do!" as if she were surprised to hear herself admit it.

This was a big insight for her. Had she been in a private dream group or individual session, I would have asked her for some examples of how she runs from her problems. I would have asked her how else she might have handled the problem, or how someone she knows and sees as more competent would have handled that predicament. This was a public forum, however, and not a place to do deep psychological work. The woman was lucky to make this connection and perhaps to plant a seed in her own mind of how she could *dream back her life* by having better coping skills in the future.

Sometimes we have a dream whose ending disturbs us because we know we died in the dream, or someone else did. We feel terrified or humiliated by the dream's distressing content. Perhaps we woke up in fright or forced ourselves awake because we felt terrified in the dream.

These dream endings leave us feeling out of control and subject to the whims of our dream machine or our unconscious. They leave us feeling out of sorts and maybe in a bad mood for several hours or more. These dream endings are signposts. Feeling out of control in a dream might be telling you that there is something in your life that feels the same way. If you do not have control of the outcome of the events of the dream, if you're feeling powerless, this is a signpost that you are feeling powerless or subject to the whims of others in your life. This is not necessarily about all aspects of your life. More likely, the emotion refers to a particular area of trouble or conflict that surfaced a day or so before you had the dream. The disturbing dream ending is a signpost to tell you that you can do something to be more in control of what's happening to you.

In general, a dream ending is a report card or a status report to tell you how you're doing at that moment. You may want to view it as a snapshot. You can make changes based on what you know about your life and what your dream is highlighting for you.

The woman whose dreams frequently end with her running away

from an assailant or a scary situation might hold that idea in her mind. She can ask herself how frequently she does this with problems in waking life. Does she ignore them and hope they'll go away? Does she pretend she doesn't have a problem at all? Does she make things worse in her denial, for example, by spending more to stifle her fears about her mounting debt? Does she say how well she is when she has actually been feeling ill? Is she frightened of being sick? Exactly and specifically, how does she run from her problems?

We each have our own styles of avoidance and denial. The dream opens the opportunity to ask these questions. Her dream behavior might be a clue to the specifics that have escaped her waking consciousness.

## CHANGING ENDINGS

One way to effectively work with dream endings is to change them. After you've already had the dream, you can change it in your imagination.

By changing a dream ending, you are consciously giving yourself a new signpost. That is, you are telling yourself that you can be more powerful, effective, and instrumental in your own life. You can alter the course of events by your own behavior, by taking desire into action. When you see yourself as competent and capable in your imagination, that attitude spills over into waking life in action. Making changes in your waking life will support your being more capable in your dreams. Waking life and dream life feed each other in a continuous loop of change and growth.

### Steps For Changing Dream Endings

1. Tell the dream to your dream partner aloud. If you don't have a dream partner, you can speak the dream out loud and tape-

record it. Or you might want to write it down in its entirety instead.

2. Tell the dream ending as it was in your dream.

3. Write a new ending to the dream. You might want to try several different endings and see which one satisfies you.

For example, if you have been chased by a monster in your dream, and your dream ends with you running away or hiding, what other endings might you make up instead? Maybe you see yourself picking up a chair and throwing it at the monster, who then cowers and gives up. Or you yell at the monster and tell it to leave you alone. You imagine yourself doing this with great competence and power. Your voice booms loud and strong and you say it like you mean it! The monster takes you seriously. Or maybe you know the monster is all bluff and you can ask it what it wants of you. You can ask aloud, "What is your message?" The response often brings surprising information.

## Working with Dream (or Fantasy) Images

1. Capture the details: size, color, light, texture, smell, position in space.

2. What emotions arise from contemplating this image?

3. What is the dominant emotion?

4. What attributes do you project onto the image (kindness, malice, joy, safety, a feeling of some special significance, and so on)?

5. How is this a metaphor or a play on words?

6. What does this remind you of?

7. What might this image symbolize for you personally?

8. How does this image fit in with the whole dream or fantasy?

9. How does the image change?

10. What in your life now is like this image and its character-istics?

11. How does the image represent a part of you?

12. What makes this image the perfect symbol for what it ex-presses?

## USING THE INSIGHTS

These signposts and endings, like all of the content of your dreams, come to bring you specific and important information. Knowing what the problem is, understanding its origins and dynamics, and knowing what you need to do are not enough. To make any of this work worth-while, you have to take the dream message into action. It is by action that you take back your life.

## DREAMS INTO ACTION

1. Make a list of your dream signposts.

2. Choose one of your dream signposts, such as an image or person, that shows up frequently in your dreams. Following the steps on pages 73–4, work with this image.

3. If this signpost is a persistent message, what is it saying?

4. How can you take this message into action?

5. How do your dreams usually end—satisfactorily or not?

6. Do you run away, give up, confront the monster, or get what you want?

7. What do your dream endings tell you about the way you usually resolve problems in your life?

8. Is there something you want to change about your style of resolution?

9. If you have an ending you don't like, use the steps for changing dream endings on pages 72–3.

10. Do a journal entry about what you have learned from your dream signposts and endings.

# CHAPTER SIX

# Conscious Dreaming

> Dreams pass into the reality of action. From the action stems the dream again; and this interdependence produces the highest form of living.
>
> —Anaïs Nin

MANY people think of dreaming as a passive event. We go to sleep. Sometimes we dream, sometimes we don't.

In fact, we dream every night, several times a night, even if we don't remember a single dream over many years. When we do remember, we may feel as if we have no control over the content or outcome of our dreams. If we don't like what happens in our dreams, we may try to block them out or deliberately distract ourselves so we won't remember them. Here are some reasons why we don't remember our dreams:

## 10 Reasons Why We Don't Remember Our Dreams

1. Dreams come to us in a jumbled, nonlinear form, which is not the way we are used to thinking. These confusing images make it difficult to relate the dream (even to ourselves) in a chronological and coherent fashion.

2. Our culture doesn't honor the dream as valuable information or take it seriously. Most people assume dreams are meaningless and see exploring them as superstitious or worse.

3. People don't pay much attention to us when we want to tell our dreams. They shrug them off and don't ask us to elaborate on the details, nor do they question what meanings the dream might hold.

4. We are often embarrassed or repulsed by the content of our dreams, so we often don't want to remember them.

5. We are afraid others will think we are crazy or weird because of the dreams we have.

6. Our nightmares frighten us and make us wonder whether we are mentally disturbed or potentially dangerous.

7. Most dreams are not emotionally charged or terrifying, so we are more likely to sleep through them without waking up. Rather, we remember the ones that are unpleasant and frightening and then dismiss them from our minds because they are so unpleasant.

8. On awakening, we begin our daily responsibilities immediately, rather than waking up slowly with time to think out what was on our minds. Dreams and nightmares are elusive and disappear on awakening if we don't make an effort to remember them.

9. Some myths about dreams discourage us from exploring them.

10. Our lives are so busy that few of us take time for contemplation of our dreams or private thoughts.

However, we can deliberately influence the content of our dreams by requesting solutions to and clarification of those issues in our lives that we find troubling. With clear intention, we can program ourselves to dream about specific subjects. The dreams that result from such incubation will offer specific answers to our dilemmas and clarify our confusion.

In this chapter, we'll review the methods to incubate dreams and explore how these consciously requested messages can be used as guides or maps for future decisions.

## INTENTION

Intention is everything.

If this sounds like hyperbole or just an overstated claim, I can only suggest you think about the times you have been successful at anything. Your intention can make all the difference between success and any other result.

> There is no chance, no destiny, no fate, that can circumvent or hinder or control the firm resolve of a determined soul.
>
> —Ella Wheeler Wilcox

When we intend to do well, accomplish something difficult, stretch ourselves into new knowledge, and overcome difficult obstacles, we often succeed. Our clear intention keeps us focused, both consciously and unconsciously, on achieving our goal. The way this focused intent works in waking life is the same way it works with dream incubation. Sincerely asking a question and being open to receiving an answer—including one you don't like—permits your dreaming self (your unconscious or higher self) to formulate the best answer. The more you can clarify the question and the more you can be open and willing to hear the answer and contemplate its many meanings, the better the dream incubation will work.

Intention includes imagining your outcome as vividly as possible, using all your senses (sight, touch, movement, smell, taste, and sound). Add any emotional flavor you'd like—great joy, bliss, pride of accomplishment, and so on.

## INCUBATING AND PROGRAMMING DREAMS

We dream about what we think about, what is on our mind during the day. What is in the foreground? Consciously, the dreamer might ask himself or herself:

What troubles me? What do I worry about? What do I fear?

What's on my mind? What are my principal concerns today?

What preoccupies my mind? What holds my energy and attention?

What am I most attending to? What am I obsessing about?

What plagues me? What haunts me?

What important solutions or decisions am I contemplating?

What should I do next?

What are my choices?

What are the significant consequences of my different choices?

In many ways, each time we go to sleep, our dreaming mind works on answering these questions. By holding *in* our minds whatever is *on* our minds as we drift off to sleep, we have unintentionally programmed ourselves to dream about this subject—and all its connecting subjects.

I use deliberate dream incubation regularly, but on one occasion (at least), I incubated a dream unintentionally. (Here I'm using the terms *incubating* and *programming* interchangeably.)

Before going to sleep, I was in bed, reading a book about eating disorders. When I read the author's warning signs of a possible eating disorder, I recognized some of my own behaviors. As I reached up to turn off the light, already close to falling asleep, I thought, *I wonder if I have an eating disorder.* Within the next ninety minutes, I dreamed.

> *I am driving my car, on the way to meet friends for an elaborate dinner at a good restaurant. I'm hungry and I have a bag of donuts (bagels?) in a bag on the passenger seat. I'm eating them one after the other, although I know that I am on my way to a big dinner and will eat that, too. I'm eating past the point of being full. In the dream, I am feeling dismayed at my behavior although I also know this isn't something I usually do. But I don't seem able to stop myself.*

I woke up almost immediately after the dream and said aloud, "I guess that answers my question." Though I hadn't intended to incubate a dream, I had followed the most important steps of dream incubation.

While I often use the terms *incubating* and *programming* interchangeably, I do see a subtle difference between them. When I think of incubating a dream, my intent resembles asking for information, using open-ended questions. When I program a dream, I am likely to be more specific. I have narrowed my search, if you will, to a specific area of inquiry or a specific problem, perhaps one that seems urgent.

- An example of an incubation question would be, "What do I need to know today about my career as a writer?"

- For a programmed dream, I might ask more specifically, "What can I do to improve my writing skills?"

---

SHARON, a visual artist, incubated a dream and asked for a dream that would clarify her feelings about her career.

*I am on an artist's retreat to do some experimental sculpting. There are a lot of stupid rules here. You can paint or sculpt only during certain hours. You have to wear special clothing on special days for each of the sculpting sessions, such as a red plaid shirt and blue slacks for the Monday morning sculpting class that starts promptly at nine. I'm late for the class and when we get there, the teacher says I'm wearing the wrong color shirt. I have to go back to change my clothes. I say, "Forget it." I'm going back, but I'm going to sculpt in my room with my own supplies.*

*In a later scene, a man at the retreat house is a special massage guru who can diagnose your problems while he gives you a massage. He's an old doctor. He barely places his hands on my shoulders and says, "You're very insecure." I say, "I'm not insecure. If my back feels tight, it's because I'm tense!" He doesn't even know me and I know I'm not insecure. He ignores me and probes further, saying that I have a weak will. "I have a very strong will! You can ask anyone who knows me. This is a fraud and I'm leaving." I get up to leave and he rushes after me. He offers me a ride home. I need a ride so I accept. He makes a sexual advance and I tell him I'm not interested. I'm not afraid of his advances, but I don't want to do this and I get out and walk back to the retreat center. I remember Peter Lawford was in line and I look for him, thinking I should have done that to begin with. Peter is gone when I get back. I wish I hadn't wasted so much time with this other man.*

In working with this dream, Sharon said that she was feeling conflicted about her career, overburdened with having to put a show on every year, and frustrated with dealing with all the details of galleries and openings. It was nearly time for her to begin preparing for the next show and she'd had a shorter hiatus than usual. The rules and details for each gallery all seemed trivial. They detracted from what she really wanted to do.

We spent some time discussing the timing of the shows, her goals for her painting exhibitions, and what Peter Lawford represented. She saw him as someone who was able to take time to play and not worry about being highly successful. When I asked what she really wanted to do, she answered quickly and with conviction: "I want to sculpt instead of paint and I don't want to have to worry about shows, reviews, or the stupid rules of the galleries."

"What else?"

"I need some more time off."

"Then take it," I said.

Sharon was visibly relieved. She said, "My body said that's the right thing to do. My shoulders just relaxed." She laughed. "I want two more months off instead of two weeks." Further discussion revealed that the doctor in the dream who was so critical was the part of herself that wouldn't let her take time off, though both her career and her finances could sustain a two-month hiatus. The incubation brought an insight into how she was being hard on herself as well as to the solution— through Peter Lawford as a symbol.

Over the next few days and after rereading her written dream, Sharon discovered several more layers of meaning. But on the night following our dream session, she had a dream that seemed to support her decision to take time off.

*I am shopping with my husband. We have a little girl with us that I don't know in waking life. She is poor—maybe an orphan. She needs new clothes and we are buying a complete outfit for her. I want to buy her new boots and a coat, too. I feel very generous and I'm enjoying this. I decide to buy her a second outfit, but she says no. She tells me not to go overboard. Enough! She's very emphatic and resists my urging to take more gifts.*

Sharon's interpretation was that the *splurge* she was allowing herself with two months off was enough. She felt as if she were spoiling her inner little girl, but she was also cautioning herself not to overdo it. Simultaneously, this dream validated her decision to take some time off.

## STEPS FOR INCUBATING DREAMS

Patricia Garfield, a well-known dreamworker and author, suggests that we incubate dreams by asking an open-ended question such as, "Tell me what I need to know." She says this kind of inquiry will yield more intriguing answers than a narrow demand. In effect, we may receive guidance in an area where we didn't think we needed it. Other open-ended questions include the following:

What is my next step?

What am I ignoring?

What is important for me to know now?

How can I be what I am meant to be?

Notice how all of these questions lack a specific focus. You might call them broad-brush questions, global questions, or life questions. They can't be answered with a simple yes or no answer.

When incubating these types of questions, you can write them on a brightly colored piece of paper and put it in your pocket or purse. Each time you reach in, you will see or feel this piece of paper and it will remind you of the question. You might read it several times during the day, holding it in your mind with intention. This keeps the question in the foreground.

You might want to do this over a period of time such as weeks or months, especially if you feel you are at a major turning point in your life or would like to be. Tracking your dreams through this time when you are ready for change and open to advice from your higher, dreaming self will help you see the choices you have available to you, what you perceive as your obstacles, and what your unconscious is telling you about overcoming them. (See Chapter 13, page 233, for help with dealing with obstacles.)

## STEPS FOR PROGRAMMING DREAMS

To use your dreams for guidance to specific problems, your questions and your focus at bedtime will help in pointing your dreaming self in the direction you want to go.

1. Ask yourself what it is exactly that you would like to know. For example, I want to know what I can do and tell myself so that I will be more at ease at parties.

2. Write out this question, using different wordings until you find the one that best captures your request for clarity and information.

3. Be specific. The question should be open-ended so that the answer is more than yes or no, but it should also focus on a specific image, idea, problem, or person—or all of these. Imagine the party where you'd like to be more at ease. What does "at ease" look like? How does it feel? Who are people who embody (literally) this impression? What do they *do and say* at parties? What can I tell myself that will help me feel more at ease? *Everyone else is nervous and shy, too. They just are better at pretending to be confident. I'm only human and it's okay to blunder.*

4. Enter this context as much as possible to ask the question— feeling as much as possible what it would be like to be *in* the context, using all five senses if possible. In the party example, I might imagine whether I'd be sitting or standing, how I can hold my body with confidence and poise, see myself smiling and making eye contact when I speak with people, taste the drink I will have in my hand, and smell the odors in the room that I associate with a party.

   For another example, if I want guidance about something related to my work, I can visualize myself working with the issue already resolved and the feelings of satisfaction of seeing, hearing, and holding the solution physically, such as the completed report or invention in my hands. The details of this kind of visualization will vary a lot between people because we have different versions of what makes something vivid. (For more suggestions on visualization, see Chapter 9.)

5. Know that you *will* dream. Remind yourself that you dream every night.

6. Before going to sleep, see yourself recording the dream when you wake up.

7. Have a means for recording or writing the dream ready at your bedside.

8. Assume that whatever you dream is an answer to your question(s).

## WHAT YOU CAN EXPECT

Expect a dream and expect an answer. The next dream you have is probably an answer to your question, although it may not appear to be an answer. Often, the dream you get after incubation seems totally unrelated to the subject matter you had in mind. Remember that dreams come in the language of metaphor and symbol. These are usually the metaphors you're likely to use in your daily speech—the same clichés that are part of your conversation habits. But they may also be brand-new metaphors and imagery that you don't recognize as your usual dreaming pattern.

More than a year ago, I incubated a dream for help with my professional life. Here is an excerpt from my journal on the dream and its first layer of interpretation.

I incubated a dream last night. Before turning off my light, I was still thinking about a possible metaphor to capture all my workshops and the skills I teach—a way to package myself for the public. I even spent some time looking at books on clichés, catchphrases, and euphemisms. On and off all day, I thought about possible ways to approach this and made some notes to check on mythology for possible sources of metaphor or imagery.

*I am at the post office, talking to Charlie, who sorts my box mail and whom I often talk to. I am trying to persuaade him to take one of my bear cubs when they are born. At home, I have a mother bear with me. I know she will deliver six baby bears in about six weeks. They will also have to be about six weeks old before they can be weaned from their mother—like puppies. The bear is in my bedroom. I think I have Charlie persuaded to take one. However, as we discuss this, I realize that when my bear delivers and the six cubs are born and start to grow, they will need a lot more space and facilities than I have for them. I can imagine that while they play they will destroy my bedroom and generally make a lot of chaos and do a lot of damage to that room. I'm a little worried about this problem, but it's more in terms of how to solve it. I seem to be confident that it's solvable. And I'm also looking forward to this event. I guess I've had this bear a long time.*

In more than a year since this dream, I have spent a lot of time working on the images of this dream. What strikes me now as I revisit it is that I remember this was a polar bear and all the work I did with it was based on its being a polar bear, not a brown or black bear with very different connotations for me. I bought books on polar bears and put up some pictures of them, pondering the possible meanings for me. Since I hate cold weather, this choice of my unconscious seemed surprising and unusual.

Here's more from my journal:

If this dream is an answer to my request for an umbrella metaphor for my work, the answer isn't clear to me yet. I hear all kinds of things as

I write this dream. And of course, I'd have to look at the homophones *bear* and *bare* and all the possible meanings. This is a job in itself. And the number six is obviously significant since it comes up three times in the dream. Maybe that's the core number of topics I should have. I have felt that there were too many all along.

First associations:

bear in the closet
bear of a problem
bare your soul
bare facts

A bear is an animal I associate with hibernation and voluntary isolation. Once again, I'm feeling that I need to go into a period of isolation or hibernation and I want to do a lot more reading than I did in this past week. This is especially true after a very social day yesterday.

So I think of bears as big, lumbering, and seemingly docile, but potentially dangerous. They are powerful. They are well adapted and sleep in caves or other cozy places. A bear's den. There was a nature show on last night and there was a segment on the polar bear and how they are so insulated that they don't even show up on heat-seeking cameras. I think of the stuffed bear at the Graves Museum on Friday night. I think of Anthony's [my ex-husband's] fascination with the ferocity of grizzly bears and his desire to hunt them. And I think of how protective a mother bear is of her cub. I know they don't have litters of cubs as mine does in the dream. This is another dream about birth, too, which seems to be a common metaphor of my speech pattern.

In the dream, my bear is a pet. I never get lucid in this dream, though I should. Having a bear as a pet is more than impractical; it's impossible. In the dream, I keep the bear in my bedroom and it's going to destroy that room—with the help of its offspring. If the bear represents my work, then perhaps I'm saying that I've brought my work into my bedroom— literally, by reading and making notes in there. And it's destroyed my sex life because I seem to have lost most of my interest and do not want a sexual partner or even a frequent companion. I want to hibernate and be alone. That's bearish.

My main feelings in the dream are excitement at the future delights of the birth of the six bear cubs. I am happy about telling Charlie this and I want to convince him of the wisdom of having one for himself when they are old enough to take. He seems as if he'd really appreciate this and I'm pretty sure he will take one. In fact, I am emphasizing he will have to wait—six weeks until birth, six more weeks until weaning.

In the time since having this dream, I've worked with it from several different angles, including the images, feelings, and associations to the elements in the dream. I played with the numbers and the time frame for birth and delivery, including the number six, which appears frequently in my dreams. (I have six more books to write?) The dream seems exceptionally rich with layers of meaning, including my identification with this pregnant female bear. In my dreams, pregnancy is usually about books I'm gestating (incubating) and ready to give birth to.

As I write this now, I have another association to other kinds of bears. On a camping trip with my ex-husband in 1971, we went to look for bears at a nearby dump. Wanting to get there before the sun went down, we left our dirty dishes from dinner on the picnic table outside our tent. When we got back after seeing bears at the dump, a neighbor camper said that a bear had come into the campsite and licked our dishes and utensils clean.

Perhaps, with this dream, I was saying to myself that I don't have to go out searching for something I want. It will come to me in its own way.

I expect more layers of meaning to this Big Dream to reveal themselves in time.

## INTERPRETING BIZARRE OR "OFF-TOPIC" DREAM ANSWERS

Frequently, incubating a dream will give an answer that seems far afield from the original question. Work the dream as you would any other. Then ask yourself how this might be an answer to the original question. The answer, as in my polar bear dream, may reveal itself over time.

Recently I was reading a book about the concept of soul loss. I pondered what that meant to me and in what ways I had experienced soul loss in my own life. I knew that when I was a child, certain desires and talents had been smothered or discouraged. I didn't think specifically about what those might be, but I knew that like most people, there were probably dozens of things that fell into this category. In my bedside notebook, I wrote:

If I have lost a part of my soul and I am ready to retrieve it, what can you, Dream Machine,* show me to help and guide me in its retrieval?

I dreamed in the first two hours of falling asleep and recorded my dream when I woke up.

A female friend (whom I don't recognize as anyone I can name) is applying for a job teaching or in administration in an educational setting. She says that part of the job application requires her to produce four years' worth of lesson plans. I tell her to do just the first year's worth in a comprehensive outline and clear details for each topic. The subsequent years can be more sketchy because she will have proven her ability to do a good job in the first year's outline. She doesn't have to do all that paperwork for all four years. As I tell her this, I'm convinced that I'm correct. I feel as if I know, without a doubt, that this will work and

---

* You may want to refer to the part of yourself that creates dreams as your unconscious, dream maker, higher self, or whatever you choose.

*she will get the job. She doesn't have to do as much as she thinks is required. She trusts my advice, which is why she has asked me.*

When I woke up, this didn't seem at all like an answer to my request. But I knew that since I had had the dream so close to my asking the question (in writing), it was likely to hold some kind of answer that wasn't apparent to me. After I discussed it with my dream partner, she said that the dream might be saying that I had asked too big a question, that the dream was offering me a shorter answer than I thought was required. "It sounds like your dream maker is saying, 'Don't ask me such a big question. One at a time is enough.'" she said.

That made sense to me. The idea was supported by the dream I had on the second night after incubation, but *before* the discussion with my dream partner.

*I am with my family members (mother, father, and sister). I discover that my father has murdered my infant nephew, Justin. I am very upset and know that I have to report him to the police—even though he is my father. It's murder! I'm afraid of him and I want to warn my mother, too. Then I see the dead baby and coo at him and he wakes up and giggles and smiles back at me. I wonder in the dream how he can be so responsive if he's dead.*

On the day preceding this dream, my nephew Justin, now an adult, had spent the day with me. I had called him to help me with a problem with my laser printer, feeling helpless and panicky when it said SER-VICE on the LCD panel. Justin's business is fixing printers and copiers, and refilling toner cartridges. He generously drove from Tampa with new parts and talked me through changing the fuser and A/C power modules, screw by screw. The next time he could ship me parts and help me do repairs by phone.

I have told myself I'm not mechanical, in spite of much evidence to the contrary. As I replaced the parts with his power screwdriver, I was surprised and pleased at how easy this felt and how comfortable I was. I even commented to Justin that this is one of my last frontiers. I often do what I fear and deliberately try to overcome those things that give me anxiety by doing them until they no longer give me such uncomfortable feelings. I would like to be more handy around my house so that I don't have to depend on others to rescue me or have to hire people to do simple maintenance tasks.

As Justin talked me through replacing the parts step by step, I remembered that I had done equivalent mechanical tasks on many occasions when I worked as a microbiologist, when I sewed all my clothes and made patterns, and later when I set up my home computer. These all required the same skills I was using with the printer repair, but I had denied myself access to them. My mechanical self isn't dead after all!

That was exactly what the second night's dream said. Clearly, the two dreams on the two nights after asking the incubated question offered answers at different depths.

If this is only one answer to such a broad-brush question, what else have I (or others in my life) killed off in me that might be akin to "soul murder"? We shall see what my dreams answer over the next few weeks while I hold this question in mind.

Astute readers will notice that another layer may reflect another kind of soul murder—my feelings about my father being a dangerous killer, even all these years after my father's death. In the dream, I blame my father for this "soul murder" of my mechanical self, symbolized by killing Justin. This lingering issue and how it influences my relationships with men in my life can also be the subject for other dream incubations. However, my father's death was a suicide, a classic murder of his own soul, which may be one of several reasons why I chose him as the killer in my dream.

Therefore, what seemed like off-topic answers in fact were very much on topic.

## 10 Steps to Improve Dream Recall

1. Keep a notebook and pen at your bedside every night and during naps if you take them. This is especially important on your days off from work, on vacation, or when you are away from home for any reason. People often recall more dreams when they are in a new or different sleep environment.

2. Go to sleep with the conscious intention of remembering your dreams. Say aloud before going to sleep: "I will dream tonight and I will remember my dreams in the morning. I'll write down my dream as soon as I wake up." Imagine yourself writing down your dreams.

3. Avoid using alarms or clock radios to wake. Upon awakening, try to stay in the same physical position in bed without jumping up.

4. Avoid alcohol and tranquilizers, both of which inhibit dreaming and dream recall. This is equally true of illegal and hallucinogenic drugs. Some medications such as antipsychotics will also reduce dreaming, but others can cause nightmares. *Consult your physician before discontinuing or reducing the dosage of any prescription drugs.*

5. Stay in bed a few minutes upon awakening and ask yourself what you were just thinking about. "Where was I? What was just happening?"

6. Write down whatever comes to mind, even if it seems completely senseless and bizarre. A short note is better than nothing at all. A fragment of a dream when recorded and reviewed will often bring back an entire dream. Dream fragments by themselves can be rich with information.

7. While still in bed, go over the dream several times in your mind to memorize the events of the dream, no matter how

bizarre or disturbing. The more disturbing or odd a dream is, the more important the message is to yourself.

8. At your first opportunity, record the dream in its entirety on paper or by tape recorder. Simply record the dream without thoughts about its interpretation or analysis. Give as many details as possible.

9. Drink a large amount of water before bedtime. When you wake up to urinate, try to capture what you were dreaming and make some notes. A few key words or phrases are often enough to help you recall your dream in the morning.

10. Be patient and keep trying. The more you want to remember your dreams and the more you pay attention to the ones you have, the more dreams you'll remember. When you have too many to record and work on, commit to working on at least one dream per week in detail.

## TROUBLESHOOTING THE ABSENCE OF DREAM ANSWERS

It's possible that you dreamed an answer but didn't remember it. In this case, follow these steps to both remember the dream and to get the answer you seek.

1. Follow the steps for improving dream recall.

2. Rewrite your question in your dream journal.

3. Do a journal entry about what obstacles you might be putting up in the way of an answer.

4. Repeat steps 1–3 for dream incubation until you get a dream.

5. Assume it's an answer—*not* "just another stupid dream."

## LUCID DREAMING

Another form of conscious dreaming is the lucid dream. When we say we are lucid in a dream, we mean that *during* the dream, we are aware of dreaming. In effect, you say to yourself *while* you are still dreaming, "Oh, if this is happening, I must be dreaming."

Since most dreams have a bizarre quality, it is surprising that we don't get lucid in our dreams more often than we usually do. I have dreams about each of my parents relatively frequently and often know in the dream that they are dead. Yet this knowledge in the dream doesn't seem to be enough to trigger lucidity. When I talk about these dreams of my parents, I say that maybe I should not be surprised that I'm not lucid in a dream where they are present, since I was never lucid around them when they were living!

In my experience, people who remember dreams and do regular dreamwork are more likely to be lucid in their dreams than those who remember dreams only rarely or who don't usually pay attention to their dreams. When we immerse ourselves in dreamwork and pay regular attention to our dreams and their signposts, we are more likely to be lucid in a dream.

However, you can cultivate the ability to be lucid in your dreams by asking yourself on a regular basis whether you're dreaming. How do you know you're really reading a book and not just dreaming you're reading a book? As you look around you, check your senses and your thinking. You will probably say that in dreams things and events are weird, your perception is fuzzy or focused in a peculiar way, or you can do things in a dream that you can't do in waking life. When you look around you, what you see now is what you think of as ordinary reality. What is the out-of-the-ordinary reality of your dreams?

Each dreamer has a particular pattern of dreaming, with regular symbols and events. Stephen LaBerge, author of *Lucid Dreaming*, calls these frequent elements *dream signs*. They can be used as reminders that we're dreaming. Sometimes this happens naturally. We realize that this event (a monster, our car flying) always happens in a dream. Then, during the dream, we think, "Oh, this must be a dream, too!"

One of the advantages of lucid dreaming is your ability to access— on the spot—the well of knowledge in the unconscious, while you are still in the dream, rather than using one of the after-the-fact techniques for doing dreamwork. You can ask the monster or the person chasing you what he wants. You can talk to the nonhuman elements in the dream (such as a wall, car, piece of paper, or creature) and tap into the meaning of the dream *while you are still in it*. This enables you to get the information the dream brings you and take it into action. You can even ask during the dream, "What action does this call for in my life?" or "What do you want me to do?"

Charles Tart, in *Conscious Mind, Sleeping Brain*, edited by Jayne Gackenbach and Stephen LaBerge, reminds us that there are degrees of lucidity. We might have a moment in a dream when we recognize a dream sign, and then forget that we are lucid and can use the information *in the dream* to take some action that would lead to further insight. During a dream I once thought, "If I'm speaking in public while wearing the ratty T-shirt I sleep in, I must be dreaming." But then the dream continued as if I didn't know I was dreaming. You might be lucid for only a moment, throughout a whole dream, or anything in between.

In many ways, the different techniques of this book are on a continuum of various kinds of lucidity—both waking and sleeping. We may be aware of our mental processes or not; we may direct them or allow them to happen passively, noticing when we want to shut them off only because we don't like the content. Lucid living is about making our unconscious thoughts more available as information to take into action, including those we have in a variety of altered states of consciousness.

## 10 Steps Toward Lucid Dreaming

1. Do reality checks. Ask yourself during the day, "Is this a dream? Am I dreaming now?"

2. Look for inconsistencies or bizarre details in your surroundings.

3. Ask yourself, "Does this feel familiar? Have I ever dreamed this before?"

4. Could these events really happen?

5. Make a habit of noticing unusual content: "These people are dead; I must be dreaming!"

6. Are there bizarre modes of transportation? If you're flying without a plane, you're dreaming.

7. Read something (a street sign, a movie marquee, or a book title). If the content changes on a second reading, you're dreaming.

8. Tell yourself you will recognize you are dreaming in the midst of your next dream. Remind yourself of this throughout the day; repeat it as you go to sleep.

9. Know that when you are lucid you will be able to alter the content of your dreams.

10. Once lucid, ask the characters who they are and what they want.


## DREAMS INTO ACTION

1. What do you need to be more effective, confident, healthy, intimate, energetic, loving, or patient? Make a list of possible choices and then pick a word that jumps out at you. Briefly, write out what this would mean. What does it look like visually? If I saw you with this change in place, what would I notice?

2. If there really were such a thing as an all-knowing guru who could answer your deepest questions about your life and your purpose, what would you ask? Be as unrealistic as you like. You are calling up the wisdom of your higher self and will likely be very pleasantly surprised at the answers. Write them down as if they were being dictated to you. Some of them may not make sense at first.

3. Program yourself to be lucid in a dream, using the following statements.

   a. While awake, I'll get into the habit of asking myself if I'm dreaming.
   b. The next time I dream about_____, I'll know it's a dream.
   c. The next time I'm having a dream, I will look around me and notice what makes it my dream reality. (See 10 Steps Toward Lucid Dreaming on pages 95–6.)
   d. I will recognize my nightmares as being dreams, not waking reality.
   e. In my dreams, I will ask the following questions (fill in your own):
      1. _____
      2. _____
      3. _____
   f. Add whatever steps will help you recognize you are dreaming.

PART TWO

# Waking Dreams

CHAPTER SEVEN

# When I Grow Up . . .

The winner of the hoop race will be the first to realize her dream, not society's dream, her own personal dream.
—Barbara Bush

As children, we all had hopes and dreams of what our futures would be like.

Perhaps you imagined yourself as having a certain kind of life, an exciting career, or the opportunities to develop the talents you knew you had. Another look at those early dreams of what you could be when you grew up can be the beginning of reshaping your waking life today—to be all you want it to be.

James Hillman speaks in the terms of his *acorn theory,* a concept that says that the seeds of our true calling and the first evidence of our authentic selves showed themselves in our childhood. He says that the acorn of childhood provides, "in a nutshell," some of the glimpses of our life calling and purpose. These early seeds from the past can be nourished today for our future growth.

## CHILDHOOD DREAMS AND FANTASIES

In Chapter 4, we looked at the sleeping dreams of your childhood. In this chapter, I ask you to think in terms of waking dreams. What did you fantasize? What were your daydreams? What did you play and imagine that pointed toward what you could be in the future?

Children often have fantasies about their futures that adults look upon as unrealistic. Children dream of being cowboys, astronauts, presidents, famous movie stars, and models. Some dream of finding the cure for a dread disease that may have touched them personally, such as a cure for cancer or AIDS that took a loved family member. They want to change the world and make a difference. Even the childhood fantasy of being a firefighter or a cowboy captures some of the grandeur the child hopes to achieve. She wants to *be somebody*, to count, to get approval and to be recognized as someone important. A friend of mine who wanted to be a firefighter is a nurse today, realizing her childhood fantasy of rescuing people.

James Hillman, author of *The Soul's Code,* says, "I want us to envision that what children go through has to do with finding a place in the world for their specific calling. They are trying to live two lives at once, the one they were born with and the one of the place and people they were born into."

We all had some version of these childhood dreams. Curtis was a little boy who built Lego cities covering his basement floor, with detail and planning on a scale that was staggering. An architect, people said. Maybe a design engineer.

But life isn't that simple. Divorce and other problems intervened to thwart Curtis's education. He didn't follow the rules. He said yes and appeared agreeable, but then would do whatever he pleased, disobeying his parents and teachers. The first signs of Curtis's opposition came early, probably before he was two, according to his family's stories. This radical difference could easily be evaluated as having an antisocial personality disorder or some other pathological diagnosis. Such negative labels often constrain a child's potential further, labeling his disobedience as badness, evil, or mental illness instead of seeing it as an indicator to full productive potential. Today, it is likely but unfortunate that a child like Curtis would be given medication to make him more docile and controllable.

Now, as an adult, Curtis uses these talents in his work with computers, but he hasn't yet found work that captures what the acorn of his childhood demonstrated. Curtis's struggles continue as he tries to make a home and family of his own. His childhood dreams still linger in his mind and show themselves in household building projects. He likes doing things, even the simple chores of everyday life, on a grand scale—a shadow of the Lego cities he built at six.

Knowing he has more talent and potential than he has used so far, Curtis can take this information into action in his life. He can use the memory and feelings of these childhood dreams to awaken that part of himself that he shelved—to go along and get along with others.

Sometimes, a teacher or coach will see the acorn in a child. The parents may be blind to a child's artistic, verbal, or physical talents and skills. Parents have their own limitations and may never consider that the next world-class physicist or choreographer could be the little child in the house who just seems weird to them. This outsider, who may become a mentor or role model, can provide the opening for a child to recognize his or her gifts, thereby altering the trajectory of the child's life.

Stephen Covey asks us to reflect on the question, "Who scripted you?" Who believed in you and encouraged you? Who mentored your development and your realizing your dreams? Who told you that you were special? A child's ability to accept such mentoring can make a big difference in later life.

## WHAT WERE THE SIGNS
## OF YOUR ACORN?

If, as a child, you imagined yourself being famous as an adult, what was in that dream? What aspect of fame was your focus? Recognition? Power? Money? Appreciation? Approval? If your dream had as its focus the reactions (shock, recognition, delight, praise, anger) of other people, you might ask yourself, "What unmet needs in my childhood was this fantasy trying to fulfill?" This, too, can point the way toward a future that will accomplish a resolution of some of the core issues in your life.

One woman who is a television reporter today says that as a child she walked around the house reading newspaper stories out loud. Another woman, a successful novelist, says that when she played as a child, she told the story of her playing to herself in third person, as if she were writing a novel.

A common dream of childhood is to be an adult, to be on our own, to be able to make our own rules and not have to be under the management of others. We imagine no longer having to keep still, silent, and well behaved, or having to hide our real feelings. A time will come when we can say no and have our way. Sometimes those who were reticent or shy as children blossom as they get older into gregarious, outgoing adults. Or the outgoing clown in childhood becomes a more contemplative, thoughtful adult. One way to look for your acorn is to look for opposites. How different are you from the child you once were? What do you want to reclaim?

## CHILDHOOD GAMES

Similarly, the games you played as a child, especially games not directed by others, can be used as insights into your acorn. When we watch children play, we detect their personality traits. We notice which children lead and direct, which ones teach, counsel, comfort, and follow others. These are early indicators not only of early training and imitation of significant adults, but also of inborn tendencies: what came inside the acorn.

A child who insists on being the teacher or the one in charge, bosses other children around, and asserts her will might have leadership qualities. These can be developed and shaped into valuable skills for dealing with others without dominating or controlling them. These signs can point the way to careers in administration, management, government, and supervision. She might be gearing up to be a movie director. That commanding child who knows how to persuade others and get them to follow may make an excellent ambassador or diplomat. Or maybe the contrary child will be our next activist, like Ralph Nader, questioning the will of other authorities such as business and government that erode our individual freedoms and put the planet at risk.

When you were a child, what kind of games did you play and what was your role in them when playing with others? If you were the kind of child who could amuse herself, who liked quiet, contemplative activities such as reading, drawing, and coloring, how are these activities mirrored in your life today? Perhaps you liked to go off and hike and explore on your own. Maybe you preferred being in a group of children, planning adventures and skirmishes. Was your play about making battles or making peace? Were you more into planning or spontaneity? Did you make up stories and tell them to your friends? Did you write poems and songs?

My recent interest in poetry has led me to talk about it with others. So many people say they read and wrote poetry as young teenagers, but never since then. What is it about turning fifteen that squelches the poet (or any kind of creativity) in us? Is that when we think we should be grown-up and serious? Is that why we suppress our acorn?

What were your favorite childhood games? Do you ever long for them? What kind of play were they? These answers might point to something missing in your life today, some way to dream back your life. How might you have those desires filled in your life today? What part of yourself did you shelve when you stopped playing your childhood games? Playing doctor might be considerably more than an example of sexual experimentation. Perhaps it was also a sign of a calling toward your life's work.

## IMAGINARY CHILDHOOD FRIENDS

All behavior is purposeful. Children create imaginary friends for a reason—to meet their needs. For some, it is a need for company because they feel isolated or have no other children to play with. For others, it meets their needs for a particular kind of company, perhaps to soothe them in some way that the real people around them do not.

For many children, an imaginary friend is a comfort and a buffer against events in their lives, a way to feel rooted and connected when life becomes unpredictable or dangerous—as life often does for each of us.

Harriet Lerner, psychologist and author of *The Dance of Deception,* tells the story of her creation of her own imaginary friend, Tony, who was from another planet. She was twelve at the time she created this elaborate tale, a time of family turmoil when her mother was diagnosed with cancer, which the family wouldn't discuss. Dr. Lerner explains how the context for this invention helps to reveal its function.

If you had an imaginary friend in childhood, you might consider how this behavior offers information about your acorn, as well as your needs at the time of the creation of this friend. Review when and how you brought your imaginary friend into being and how this might be a split-off part of yourself. What did an imaginary friend offer you that you needed then? What might it offer you now?

## DRESS-UP

When you were a child, you probably loved dressing up. Whether the dress-up was for a real occasion or an imaginary one such as a tea party, dressing up meant taking on a new persona. Often this persona was one that wasn't available to you as a child, one that felt more adult, important, beautiful, or wise. By wearing someone else's clothing or jewelry, you could magically take on his or her attributes of power, class, or skill. Like Superman, wearing a cape imparted supernatural powers.

Changing appearance as a way to enter into another realm is an ancient custom of all cultures and religious traditions. Children do this naturally, wearing Mommy's shoes and makeup or Daddy's tie and hat.

It is a way to literally try on the role, to practice being the adult version of your gender or its opposite. Childhood games are normal, but they are also revealing. As an adult, you can look back on your own exploration of dress-up with clothes from old trunks in an attic or basement. What were you drawn to in dressing up as a child that brought out some aspect of yourself that might be lost to you now? If you ever cross-dressed as a child (and most children do), what were you trying to discover? Did being an adult in the opposite gender offer something you knew you would miss? Little boys often feel inadequate because they will never have babies. Little girls recognize the power and prestige that boys have, seemingly based on their gender alone.

Costumes for Halloween are another kind of dress-up. The costumes and masks you wore as a child or longed to wear are more clues to hidden parts of yourself. Some of those parts are concealed by the adult persona you wear now. What do those old costumes tell you about yourself? One person's list of costumes included a ballet dancer, a speed-skater, and a trapeze artist. This reflected a desire to be physical and body-centered in a graceful, accomplished way, reminding her of how much she missed participating in physical challenges.

## CHILDHOOD VISIONS OF ADULTHOOD

Children sometimes have visions of what their adult lives will be like. Your vision then, especially compared with what your life is like now, will tell you something of what those early callings were. One of the things I imagined was that I would have a house in the country, on property with an expanse of lawn and lots of shade trees. That image still calls to me and has been minimally appeased by where I now live. It's a reminder to spend more time in nature, surrounded by trees. By walking and spending time in a state park close to my home, I can satisfy this desire.

As a child, I wanted to sing and dance and I wanted my family members to watch and praise me. Today, my public speaking is a vestige of that acorn. My mother told me I talked too much and I was a big dreamer. Now I get paid to talk about dreams.

Was your acorn disparaged as a child? How have you turned that acorn into an asset? How can you do that now?

When we rekindle the hopes and dreams of our childhood, we can also resurrect their attributes that were obscured and discouraged as we grew up. We can return to the openness, joy of learning, trust, play, experimentation, exuberance, spontaneity, awe, and wonder—those traits referred to as "beginner's mind" in Zen.

Do you have a cynical attitude about life experience not being new or fresh? How might you recapture your childhood joy and wonder at the magnificence all around you?

We may shrink from this with anxiety. Thomas Moore, in his book *Care of the Soul,* reminds us that this return means we have to face "the vast range of our incapacity." We like to think of ourselves as competent adults, in control of our lives. A return to childhood experiences and ways of thinking can upset our equilibrium in productive ways that open us to self-exploration.

## DREAMS INTO ACTION

1. List the childhood games that you liked best. Consider board games, team sports, cards, or games of imagination. What patterns do you notice?

2. What solitary games or hobbies did you like as a child?

3. When playing with other children, what role did you naturally gravitate toward as a child (for example, leader or follower, teacher or pupil)? What does this tell you about yourself that you didn't know before you asked this question?

4. If you had an imaginary friend, what needs did it meet?

5. In your journal, engage in a dialogue with your imaginary friend and ask it questions to reveal information about your acorn. (If you didn't have an imaginary friend, you can make one up now for this exercise.)

6. What are your acorns?

7. Go to a toy store and wander around. Notice what you're drawn to, what kinds of toys you'd like to play with. Buy something you really want and PLAY with it.

8. Ask an older family member what he or she remembers of you as a child. What did he or she notice about your character and calling?

9. Make a list of all the Halloween costumes you've worn (or wanted to wear). What does this list tell you about yourself? Which one would you love to wear again?

10. Go to a thrift store or two, especially ones that are not in your neighborhood. (In another neighborhood, you are likely to find different ethnic groups or economic classes.) Wander around the clothing racks and see what draws you. You might want to buy yourself something—especially if you're thinking you'd *never* go to a thrift store. They're great places to assemble Halloween costumes, too.

11. Do exercise 10 as someone else—the person you'd like to be, a character in a novel you've read, or a character in a novel you'd like to write. How does this feel? What did you discover about yourself?

# CHAPTER EIGHT

# Daydreams, Fantasies, and Imagination

I dream for a living.

—Steven Spielberg

JUST as certain symbols in our night dreams are signposts toward our most positive future, our waking fantasies and daydreams can be viewed as indicators of our purpose and true self. These flights of fancy reveal our longings and our passions, allowing us to have a glimpse of their possible fulfillment. When we pay attention to these mental excursions, we can see how they can be looked at as we would a night dream. They contain messages of our needs, desires, hopes, and wishes. Fantasies can reveal what is missing from our lives and may show us how we might include what we long for.

In general, Western culture disparages fantasy and daydreams. Children are scolded in school for daydreaming. They are told they are being inattentive and are wasting time, and are punished by being called on when the teacher knows they weren't listening. The assumption is that daydreaming is a kind of mental doodling and therefore unproductive. Adults punish themselves for daydreaming, referring to their reveries as woolgathering, thereby ridiculing the practice as well as the content. We feel guilty when our minds wander, when we are "spacey" or can't hold our focus. Or we say we are building castles in the air and believe this inattentiveness is somehow bad. At best, we attribute our daydreaming to having too much on our minds or not enough on our minds that is important to us. We might believe the tendency comes from being tired. In its worst form, self-criticism about fantasies might include accusations of being a worthless bum or concern that the content betrays our character flaws.

In fact, fantasies are one of the ways we keep ourselves in balance. In them, as in our dreams at night, we try on new behaviors, practice future conversations, or rewrite the dialogue for old ones that left us unsatisfied. In fantasy and with hindsight, we have that witty comeback we missed in the moment. Fantasies, even those of revenge, have a kernel of hope that our lives could be better. The fantasy allows us to get what we want, be right, and attain justice.

## FUNCTIONS OF DAYDREAMS AND FANTASIES

Our inner life of daydreams and fantasies serves many important functions. Daydreams:

- Satisfy desires, including forbidden ones

- Provide entertainment

- Express emotion

- Allow us to mentally try out and practice new behavior

- Turn us on sexually

- Stimulate us mentally

- Allow us to examine new ideas

- Create a vision for our future

- Redo and undo events from the past

- Plot a course of future action

- Change our mood (calm, soothe, excite, reassure, validate)

- Prepare us for a new situation

- Distract us from a painful present

- Solve problems and find solutions

- Anticipate the consequences of various courses of action

- Integrate new information

- Justify or validate a particular decision

- Allow us to negotiate between our conflicting feelings

Fantasies and daydreams might be about:

- Relationships

- Work and success

- Self-image

- Body image

- Spiritual development

- Fame

- Power

- Money

- Leisure and solitude

Fantasies and daydreams may include conversations or arguments we'd like to have with certain people, telling them what we have been unable to communicate. As we fantasize, we mentally rehearse the right words and prepare ourselves for the possible ways others will react. Or we may imagine getting the reactions we want: approval, praise, acceptance, and agreement.

A particular fantasy may contain the elements of an ideal spiritual retreat we desire, the kind of working environment that would be ideal, or the public recognition that would be a balm to the wounds and slights of our past—personally and professionally. These little fictions reveal what is unfinished and unfulfilled.

In her book *By Force of Fantasy,* Ethel Person says, "Fantasy, no matter how remote it may be from our actual life or who we appear to be on the surface, means something, tells us something about who we are—if only we can find the courage to contemplate it and the psychological insight to decipher it. Through our fantasies we may glimpse our desires and sometimes our most authentic self-portraits."

By tracking the subjects you fantasize about, you can learn something of your most passionate desires. What is important to you, what you need to do next and are ready to do, your style of coping and solving problems are all revealed in your fantasies. When we catch ourselves daydreaming, we are likely to shake them out of our head (sometimes with a literal shake of the head) and then forget where we went mentally. By paying attention to them, we can learn a lot about ourselves without having to pay someone else to tell us the patterns they see.

*To track your fantasies, notice when your mind wanders.*

Driving is a time when many people have fantasies, but any repetitive, mechanical activity will be a good time to notice where your mind goes. This is also a good time to notice creative urges that float to the surface, since they come from the same source as fantasies and nighttime dreams.

Other common times for fantasies are when we are waiting somewhere—in line at the supermarket, before a meeting or event begins, *during* boring meetings at work, or other times that don't seem to require our full conscious attention or demand our performance and activity. Of course, driving should be in the category of times when we *are* giving our full attention, but it's easy to "zone out" when driving; most of us have had that experience. As you bring yourself back to attention, ask yourself what you were thinking about.

Household chores are another time we wander off mentally. Some people actually say they like housework because they can let their mind wander where it will without any danger. Dusting, folding laundry, and washing pots and dishes are good times for reverie. So are the times when we are watching television, but not really listening or taking in the images in front of us.

If you don't think you fantasize, you might ask yourself what you think about when you hang out in bed, take a walk, or do any of the previously mentioned activities. Where does your mind go? Are you focused more on sensual, physical experience than thoughts? Are you replaying memories and not considering them fantasies? Beginning meditators quickly discover what an active fantasy life they have!

Once you make a habit of noticing where your mind goes in fantasy, you will likely notice repeating patterns, symbols, and characters—just as in your nighttime dreams. You will also notice that you have preferred modes of experience in your fantasy. You may have a preference for dialogue and imaginary conversations over adventures and action. Or perhaps your fantasies are frequently about some peaceful place you have experienced or invented, as a way to take you away from the stress of your everyday life. This is not a bad thing! Later in this chapter, we'll look at techniques to have a place in your mind to take you away from it all when you need to do just that, but can't hop in the car and go to a retreat in the country.

Monitor your fantasy life for a few days and make notes in a pocket notebook. What is your style of fantasy? What subjects come up repeatedly? What do these reveries tell you about yourself? How do they call for action?

Ethel Person says that in the preconscious—the part of our minds that is not fully in awareness—much problem solving occurs. "There the job of modifying current cultural scripts to suit our own purposes, our underlying wishes and needs, takes place; in the laboratory of the preconscious we fashion our rehearsal (or preparatory) fantasies, fantasies that may be actualized. All of us are creative to some extent in spinning fantasies as guides that hold out the possibility of future gratification."

## Suggestions for Tracking Fantasies and Daydreams

1. Notice when and where you are most likely to fantasize and have daydreams. (Driving? In the shower? Doing certain repetitive chores?)

2. What emotions trigger your fantasy life?

3. What circumstances (people, places, and so on) trigger certain fantasies?

4. What emotions do these fantasies create?

5. Devise a system for catching these fleeting daydreams (for example, making notes or keeping a handheld voice-activated tape recorder in the car).

6. What patterns do you see?

7. How do these waking dreams serve you? What do they do for you?

8. How do your fantasies arouse, soothe, or stimulate you?

9. How do your fantasies contribute to or *fuel* your moods?

10. How do your fantasies provide justification for your behavior?

11. What fantasies come up most often?

12. During which fantasies do you most lose track of time or awareness of your current surroundings?

## WHERE YOUR MIND GOES

In the following suggestions, it's important to notice exactly where your mind goes in a fantasy. To a place? To a person? To a particular emotion or sensory experience that you have had in the past or would like to have? Do you want more of something or less? What is the focus? Nearly everyone has had a fantasy about winning the lottery or coming into great wealth some other way. As with any particular dream image, what extra money means to someone is very individualized and idiosyncratic. For different people, the meanings can be completely different—greed and hoarding, generosity and charity, or security and freedom. The details of your fantasies will reveal what is distinct and unique for you. They tell you about your callings, even while your mind and body are involved in other activities.

## HOBBIES AND AVOCATIONS

Our hobbies, too, offer information about our personal talents and passions. Any of these might be guides to changes we are ready to begin to make our lives happier. These same indicators may have the seeds of a future profession we would like to pursue. Many people dismiss a hobby as something they could never make a living at, following the "Don't quit your day job" slogan. While it may be true that your hobby might not be enough to support you financially, it can tell you something about yourself and your needs that might not be in full consciousness—especially if you have never looked at your hobby as a source of information about who you are.

If you believe that your hobby is personal and private, that is a further indication that this activity offers you a psychic nurturing that is outside the scope of your other activities. While a hobby doesn't have to be an addiction, it may have similar attributes to addictive behavior. That is, we do the behavior because it fills a need. (All behavior is purposeful.) What is its function? What's the payoff? What does it give you? How does it serve you?

Again, do note that I ask this question as a way for you to make a personal discovery, not so that you can put (more) negative labels on yourself about why you do things—seeing them as signs of neurosis, hostility, or insecurity. The diagnostic path leads to telling yourself what's wrong with you, to what you "should" or shouldn't do. This inquiry is more about finding out how your mind works and consciously using *what already works* for you.

More than one person who loves to bake cookies has turned it into a million-dollar business. Many people have discovered that an artistic or household project can be transformed into a business.

## WINNING THE LOTTERY

Many people have fantasies of winning the lottery. In my workshops, I sometimes ask people to indulge in this fantasy as a way of clarifying their values. What first comes to mind about a financial windfall can tell you about what is most important to you or what is missing most in your life—at least on that day. If your first thought is about buying conspicuous possessions (a Ferrari, a yacht, a private plane), why do you want to own these things? What is your focus—what other people will see, how it will make them envious or happy for you, or how you will enjoy these items? How does this contrast with your life without lottery winnings? If you could spend it only in ways that were not conspicuous, what would you do?

For some people, winning the lottery means that they will have the freedom to do things they feel they can't do now. Perhaps they believe their time and energy are taken up with working most of their waking hours at a job, shopping, cooking, cleaning, taking care of a house and car, and other chores, all of which keep them from doing what they most like to do. If your leisure is limited and you get to play golf or read a book too rarely, winning the lottery might mean that you can pursue these pleasures more often. Perhaps this large amount of money would free you from a relationship where you feel stuck. Asking a couple with relationship problems what each would do if he or she won the lottery can sometimes reveal that the relationship is held together more for financial security and fear than out of mutual desire and appreciation.

One woman said that if she had that much of her own money, she'd leave her husband in a heartbeat. Rather than seeing this as a sign of her greed, it served as a window on her unhappiness. She could then ask herself what she could do to improve the relationship so that she would want to stay no matter how much money she had.

The fantasy of winning offers a view of what might be the more important issues in someone's life.

If you won the lottery, what would you do? Would you give any money away? To whom? Why? What do these answers tell you about yourself?

## THAT LITTLE RUSH

Some fantasy material is more shadowy or elusive than a fantasy we can monitor with conscious intent. You may see something that gives you a little rush of glee or a pleasant glow. The exact origins of the rapid series of emotions may be complex and hard to entangle, but there's an unmistakable tingle at certain sights, sounds, or thoughts. One woman said she got a kind of glowing feeling whenever she saw a man driving with his dog in the passenger seat. The details revealed it was usually a young man alone, most often driving a truck, and she assumed he was on his way to work at a job in construction or some other physical, outdoor, macho kind of job. She saw his dog as a constant companion, representing loyalty. For her, it also represented his ability to make a loving connection with another living being. She felt especially warm and fuzzy if he leaned over and spoke to the dog or patted it as he drove. She could make what felt like a heart-to-heart connection to this total stranger because of what she imagined his relationship to his dog to be.

Another person said he got a little rush every time he drove past a university campus. Those brick buildings gave him a little sensation of excitement—almost like sexual arousal, he said. Wondering whether he wanted to be a student or a teacher, I asked what he imagined when he saw these buildings. His answer revealed that he wanted both. He regretted not finishing college, and that little rush of excitement kept calling him back. He always wanted to teach as well. This little clue opened several possibilities for this young man's future.

## DOODLING AND DRAWING

We've all found ourselves doodling on a notebook or the blotter on our desk when we were in school. For some, doodling comes naturally, something to do on paper placemats in restaurants, in the margins of phone books while we're on hold waiting, or on advertisements in magazines. What do you draw? Do you have a favorite doodle that you repeatedly use? We usually think of these as meaningless, and we object when others try to analyze them and tell us what they mean. Such comments feel critical and intrusive, as they often are, especially if we didn't solicit these opinions. Such interpretations, as when others insist on telling you what your dream means, say more about the interpreter than about the doodler or dreamer. But you might want to examine your own doodles and spontaneous drawings to see what you can discover. What is your interpretation? Under what circumstances are you likely to make these doodles? Do you see a pattern in style and timing emerging?

## HOT BUTTONS

What drives you crazy? Makes you furious? Rather than leading to anger, your hot button might trigger some other strong emotion such as despair, helplessness, or fear. Hot buttons bring on strong emotions, including good ones such as joyful and ecstatic feelings. What does it for you? What puts you over the edge? What moves you? What touches your heart?

If these questions sound a bit sexual, you're not off the mark. Sexual passions are often related to other passions in our lives; we frequently use similar language and metaphors to express strong emotions of all kinds:

"That makes me hot."

"I'm juiced!"

"Go for it!"

Your hot buttons tell you something about what is very important to you. At some point, you might want to change the importance of any particular item after you're more aware of how strongly you react. But for a start, notice what your hot buttons are. What makes you lose it—what moves you to tears or anger or a desire to help? What sends you careening into strong emotions of tenderness and affection—sometimes toward a stranger? What dips you into ecstasy? What melts your heart?

When we read a book or watch a movie, we are sometimes moved in ways we don't expect. Sometimes a poem, sculpture, or painting will move us to tears and we can't even begin to say why.

You may wonder why a particular photo in the newspaper or a report on television—even a commercial, when you know your emotions are being manipulated—can trigger a strong emotional reaction. Immediately, you may want to write a letter or a check; you may want to join the protest and march with a sign. Even if you've never followed through to *do* any of these things, you've probably had those moments when you fleetingly thought you would. What are the circumstances that grab you and jerk you out of your complacency, out of your daily trance?

Other hot buttons are topics or words that offend you, all those things that make you recoil in revulsion. Of course, they show up in our nighttime dreams, but they are often thrust on us by others in public places and in the media. What makes you close your eyes to block out the image? What makes you want to leave a room, put your fingers in your ears, change the television channel, or hide under the covers?

When a particular word is a hot button, you can use this experience for self-understanding, just as you would an element in a dream. You can ask yourself the same questions:

What does this word mean to me?

What does it make me think of?

What does it remind me of?

How are these emotions familiar?

What action does it call for?

What hidden aspect of myself does this emotion reveal?

What part of myself am I rejecting?

When a person drives you crazy, you might ask yourself how he or she is a mirror for you. Perhaps you do the same things as this person. If you have moved beyond the level of this person's struggle, if you no longer get yourself into the messes this person does, you might consider that he or she reminds you of where you have been—and oh so recently! Robert Kegan, author of *In Over Our Heads: The Mental Demands of Modern Life*, notes that there is nothing so unattractive as the stage of development you have just left.

Your hot buttons are important signposts, just as the recurring images of our dreams are signposts. The emotional reactions are calls to a deeper experience of meaning and purpose in the world. This is true whether they trigger strongly positive or negative emotions.

A friend of mine was with her husband, about to record their outgoing message on their answering machine. Her husband suggested they use his voice rather than hers as a way to announce she was not a woman living alone in the city. While this made perfect sense to her *logically,* her emotions objected strongly enough to cause her to cry out of anger. For her, the suggestion brought up all her feelings about being vulnerable as a woman, the sexism she experienced in her profession, and the awareness of her own volatility. From such a simple interaction, she and her husband were able to discuss (again) their feelings about power and safety.

Sometimes, strong emotions obscure a deeper layer of contrasting or opposite feelings. If I am jealous of my lover's attention to someone else and I get angry, I might be reacting in ways I am programmed by society to react. This might obscure other feelings of being turned on and excited by watching him flirting with someone else. If I am deeply grieving a loss, I might be unable to see how this setback was one I longed for at some level. My emotions may include relief as well as grief.

## WHAT DO YOU COMPLAIN ABOUT?

Everyone complains. We complain about all kinds of things, including circumstances we have no control over, such as the weather. Some people have a litany of complaints running through their heads on a regular basis. But we all have our pet peeves. What do you complain about? If you are contained and you don't complain openly, what do you think about that might be a silent complaint?

Our complaints—even about the weather—tell us something about what we find distracting and offensive. They are telling us what changes we need to make if we would only listen. If you continually complain about the weather, you might consider the possibility that you are living in a climate that doesn't suit you. If you complain about feeling stressed and overworked, what changes can you make? We say people don't listen to our complaints, but often we don't listen to ourselves.

## PRIVATE PASSIONS

All of us have private passions. These may be pleasures we talk about or those we consider more personal and secret. Private passions don't have to be concealed, however, to reveal to you some aspect of your calling. This treasured love might be a candidate for expansion into a life purpose or new career. The passionate interest will offer information about you that might not be revealed otherwise.

Here are some examples of private passions:

- Watching wrestling on television

- Reading mysteries (To figure out "whodunit," like a puzzle? To learn how they are written so you can write one? To escape from your daily boredom?)

- Watching people at airports (What are you observing? Clothing? Interpersonal communication? What they are doing? Are you assessing their physical health and how they carry their bodies? Do you make up stories about their lives and their destinations?)

- Collections (from dolls to guns)

- A special interest in a culture or place and its art and architecture

- A special interest in an era's politics, art, or social consciousness (reading books about the 1890s or the 1960s, for instance)

What do you collect? What would you like to collect? Think about these items and what attracts you to them. What emotional state do they create in you? Is having them enough or is it important that other people know that you have the largest collection of wingdings on the planet? If the items are from a particular culture or era, what do you admire most about them? What is embodied in these items? What does owning them mean to you? What do they symbolize?

## CRAVINGS AND LONGINGS

What do you crave? What do you long for? These yearnings can sometimes be reinterpreted as an urging toward the satisfaction of some need. The need will be more than the superficial layer we see. For example, people who overeat often eat past being satisfied. On the first layer, they like to eat; they enjoy food. But if you're eating and you're not really hungry for food, Geneen Roth, in her book *Feeding the Hungry Heart: The Experience of Compulsive Eating,* suggests you ask yourself, "What are you hungry for?" Sometimes the craving—whether for food or to sit by a fire or anything else—highlights some unmet need. The actual desire is the first layer of meaning, often a literal one, as is layer one in dreamwork. Beneath it are the metaphorical layers that the longing may symbolize. If I'm sleepy, I may need rest. But that longing for sleep may also be telling me I need to go inward or be alone and be quiet.

When you have a sudden craving for something such as going shopping or munching on a candy bar, what comfort are you seeking? What state are you trying to change? Are you trying to increase or decrease your level of stimulation? What will be satisfied by this act? Will engaging in this behavior cause you to feel worse?

Pay attention and discover what this craving is telling you *before* you satisfy it automatically. It may be a symbol for some important need that has been unfilled in your life—perhaps for all of your life so far. This can be the time to make a change. Even a small clue can be used for a big change.

A woman who found herself wanting to buy new clothes every winter realized that what she really missed was light and color. That insight sent her outdoors for images to paint instead of to the shopping mall.

## ROMANTIC FANTASIES

The stereotype is that only women have romantic fantasies, but both men and women have them—perhaps more frequently than they generally admit. Like all fantasies, we have romantic fantasies to satisfy a need, to mentally practice a behavior, or to create an emotional and physical state that will prepare us for something else. An example would be creating a preferred kind of romantic fantasy to lead into sexual arousal for a sexual encounter. Some people don't need the romantic component for sexual arousal, but some people do.

Whether you are in a relationship or not, romantic fantasies are normal. (Not having them is also normal.) Like all our fantasies, we create them for a reason. The romantic fantasies you conjure up will give you some insight into yourself. What do these stories tell you about yourself? What is the setting? Who is present? What feelings and memories does the fantasy call up? What needs does it satisfy?

Relationships, no matter how good they are, always fall short of our ideal. Other people have their own desires and needs (imagine that!) that sometimes conflict with our own. In a fantasy, we're in charge of content, pacing, every word and action, and the emotional reactions we want others to have—for our benefit. The fact that reality can never match our fantasies is not a reason to stop having them. The kind of specific fantasies about relationships we have can narrow the focus. They can suggest solutions to problems that seem hopeless or overwhelming. A single fantasy might reveal something that we can take into action with a partner now or in the future. We can, in fantasy, practice asking for what we'd like. We can imagine the setting and mood of a future encounter.

What are your romantic fantasies like? Is there something in them that would embarrass you to tell someone else? Would you dare to share them with your partner? Why or why not? Too mushy? Maybe your partner would like the same thing! You won't know if you don't share it.

## SEXUAL FANTASIES

Most people have sexual fantasies, though there are those who aren't sure they do. When asked about their fantasies, some people say they don't have them, but when asked more specifically about what they think of before or during sex, they realize they do have some version of a sexual fantasy. The fantasy may be simply imagining and anticipating what you would like to do in the present sexual encounter. It may have a purely sensate focus without a story or even a particular activity.

Sexual fantasies can be divided into several types:

- Things you have done before and replay in your mind because they still excite you

- Things you imagine you would do if you had the opportunity

- Things you would never do—but it turns you on to think about them

- Sexual things you can't let yourself think about—but they pop into your consciousness against your will

- Some combination of these

Your sexual fantasies can tell you about your sexuality, your unmet needs and desires. They may even reveal information on a symbolic level, as an expression of power, hostility, or the longing to incorporate some trait of the person who is a sexual partner in the fantasy. By observing the specific content of your sexual fantasies, you can observe what you like best and consciously add it to your behavior. You may decide to share the fantasy with a lover as part of foreplay.

Most people have a favorite set of fantasies to help them focus on sex when they want to be sexual—whether alone or with a partner. They use the fantasy as a mental movie to turn themselves on. Most people have a set of fantasies that provide a personal library to draw from, offering them the images, sounds, behaviors, and interactions that are most sexually stimulating. Knowing what fantasies contribute to your arousal and orgasm can ensure more consistent orgasms as well as offering you better communication with a partner. Paying attention to these preferences so that you can call them up at will can improve your sexual satisfaction. Having a repertoire of sexual fantasies can improve your solitary sex when your partner is unavailable, unwilling, or when you simply prefer to masturbate. If you like, you can use erotic books and magazines for other more interesting fantasies.

If your sexual fantasies worry you because you feel they are inappropriate or immoral to your standard of ethical behavior, remind yourself that there is a big difference between the thought and the deed. You can fantasize about doing something that might be dangerous in real life, knowing that in the fantasy you have complete control over what other people do and the outcome of the fantasy. There are no negative consequences to these mental encounters, unlike what might happen if you did them in reality. They can't hurt anyone as long as you don't do them.

In fantasy, you don't have to be politically correct or worry what others might think. You might choose a sexual partner who appeals to you physically, but whom you consciously dislike as a person. You can imagine all kinds of combinations of partners who might be inappropriate because they are otherwise committed or dangerous in some way. In fantasy, you don't have to worry about the real consequences of disease, pregnancy, being hurt, or getting arrested.

What sexual fantasies do you enjoy on a regular basis? Do they suggest any change in your behavior? Can you share them with an intimate partner?

What sexual fantasies do you not allow yourself? Why not? What do you tell yourself that prevents you from enjoying them? What do you fear?

Remember that part of having a sexual life that is satisfying and comfortable means making friends with your mind *and* body. It means trusting yourself and your desires, with the confidence that you will act responsibly.

## ENVY AND JEALOUSY

Whom are you envious of? What makes you jealous? These emotions are often the dark side of admiration. We wish we had these same successes and so we feel angry that others have achieved them. We may feel we are more talented, educated, and knowledgeable, and their success seems unfair. However, these feelings are clues to our own longings. Whom do you envy? Why?

## MORBID OR SELF-CRITICAL FANTASIES

Some people complain that when they allow themselves to fantasize or just allow their minds to wander, they have morbid fantasies. They see past unpleasant events or they imagine catastrophes and disasters of all kinds. Such thoughts can lead to worries and more fantasies that are morbid. They then find themselves in emotional distress, with anxiety and depression spiraling out of control. They may become afraid of their thoughts as well as the nightmares that are ready to surface again.

At such times, remember that the fantasies you create for yourself have a reason that you, on some level, know. (All behavior is purposeful.) You might ask yourself how these fantasies serve you. Do they keep you safe in your stuckness? Are they an excuse not to take your life in your own hands?

Jack Kornfield, in *A Path with Heart,* says, "When any experience of body, heart, or mind keeps repeating in consciousness, it is a signal that this visitor is asking for a deeper and fuller attention." What attention might that be in your circumstances?

Some people, when monitoring the content of their thoughts and fantasies, also complain of hearing a constant barrage of criticism. They may be inclined to say that these are only the tapes of critical parents, teachers, and supervisors. However, blaming these other people keeps us unaware of how *we have installed* their messages. We play them over and over again in a continuous loop. When we become aware of doing it, we can stop. We are merely perpetuating the criticism of others by doing this same behavior to ourselves.

One way to confront this continual tape is to open a dialogue with this critical voice. What is it saying? How do you want to respond? Know that by doing this exercise, you are really having a discussion with parts of yourself—even if the critical words seem to be from people in your past.

Jack Kornfield reminds us that we can find peace and compassion only when we stop the war we have with ourselves. When we stop hating our bodies, thoughts, and feelings, we can accept them as they are, especially when we find them distasteful. We can be open to what they have to teach us about ourselves.

## FANTASY AND MEDITATION

Some styles of meditation suggest that you notice your thoughts as they come, noting them as "I'm (judging, thinking, feeling, and so on)," and see these mental processes as only thoughts (or feelings) and let them go. The intent is to get out of your head, stop analyzing, and move away from intellectual processes that keep you stuck. Rather than making note of these thought processes, you can use them to learn something about yourself when you see their repeating patterns. These thoughts, some of which may seem intrusive, may also be an indication of an inner calling.

If you find in meditation that your mind frequently goes to criticism of others, what does this tell you about yourself? What does it say about your need to criticize? Is this commentary more appropriately applied to yourself? Are you dealing with your own feelings of inadequacy by focusing on your perception of inadequacy in others?

> There's a kind of illumination in the meditation aware-
> ness process that's very much like doing therapy for one-
> self, simply by listening and paying attention. These
> insights and the acceptance that comes with nonjudg-
> mental awareness of our patterns promote mental balance
> and understanding, so it can lessen our neurotic identi-
> fication and suffering.
>
> —Jack Kornfield

But we must take these insights into action—in our daily lives—for them to be truly therapeutic. "Daydreaming per se does not help you build adaptive resources and does not prepare you for the future. You must process your daydreams to gain fresh insights and under-standing if you want to be able to better cope as life goes on," says Robert Langs in his book *The Daydream Workbook: Learning the Art of Decoding Your Daydreams.*

## FANTASY AND THE SHADOW

One way to look at the unpleasant thoughts and fantasies that come to mind is to know that this is another part of us—a part that proves our humanity and imperfection. Making friends with our shadow makes us less likely to act out our hostile and aggressive impulses. We know ourselves and we have a good sense of who we are on a deeper level.

Knowing you're having a hostile reaction toward someone makes you able to be with this feeling, separating the emotion from the deed. What you *feel* is very different from what you *do* with your feelings.

We always have a choice about taking any feelings into action—after evaluating our goals and the consequences of our behavior.

## DREAMS INTO ACTION

1. Make a list of the times you find yourself fantasizing. When do you do it the most? In bed? While traveling? Use this information to create situations in which you give yourself permission to do this ordinary daydreaming for the purpose of tracking content and style.

2. List the subjects you fantasize about. Do you notice a pattern you haven't seen before?

3. What are your hobbies? Especially list those hobbies that you used to do and no longer take the time for. Make a list of all the hobbies you've ever had, including those you haven't gotten to yet, but would like to explore. What does this tell you about yourself?

4. If you won ten million dollars in the lottery, what would you do as soon as you found out? Whom, if anyone, would you tell first? What would you do? How might it change your life? For better or for worse? Would you give any of the money away? Why or why not? How do you decide how much and whom to give it to? Do you want to attach conditions and controls onto the use of the money, or is it a free gift?

5. What gives you a little rush? Notice those moments when you are out and about. What gives you that little glow of

happiness similar to the one described by the woman who liked to see men driving with their dogs?

6. What do you crave? Make a list in as many areas of your life as you can think of, not just food cravings. What are you hungry for?

7. Doodle. Take a small sketchpad and doodle as often as you can for the next week. How does that feel? What comes up for you?

8. What are your hot buttons? What sends you off the deep end? Write about the first three things that come to mind. Do you see a pattern?

9. Make a list of your private passions, past and present. What do you notice? Do you see a pattern or a common thread? What passion would you like to indulge in but hold yourself back? Why?

10. Write out a romantic fantasy. You might use the format of a fairy tale or tell it as if it were about someone else. "There once was a woman who . . ." What do you discover?

11. Write a sexual fantasy. What do you notice? Is there something in the fantasy that you would like to do? Or does this fantasy work for you because you know it's safe as a fantasy?

12. How do you make the distinction between the fantasies you'd like to do and those that are best left as fantasies?

13. What body signals, thoughts, and beliefs tell you the difference between these different kinds of fantasies?

14. Whom do you envy? When are you jealous? What do these feelings tell you about yourself?

CHAPTER NINE

# Creative Visualization and Guided Imagery

Champions are made from something they have deep inside them—a desire, a dream, a vision. They have to have the skill, and the will. But the will must be stronger than the skill.

—Muhammad Ali

THE popular techniques of creative visualization and guided imagery can offer us opportunities to see our lives through a different window. By having another vision of ourselves in new and imagined circumstances, we can free ourselves of our old restraints. This opens new possibilities for who we are and who we can be.

Creative visualization may be active or passive. Of course, like lucid dreaming and other techniques discussed in this book, the method can be seen as being on a continuum with various degrees of conscious direction and thought. In addition, because many of us find our lives very busy, we feel stressed. We may find it difficult to relax or retreat from the whirl of tasks and responsibilities. Creative visualization provides a way to take a miniretreat anywhere and anytime, without cost or risk. We can always have a safe place to go in our minds while remaining in the world as required of us.

Visualization has become quite popular at talks and workshops. It may be either active or passive. Each type has its own value, but you may have a preference.

## PASSIVE VISUALIZATION

In the passive form of creative visualization, you allow your mind to wander naturally from a simple limited focus, such as a peaceful setting of your choosing. From that mental space, you let go of the conscious control of your thoughts, emotions, and associations. You allow them to go where they will. You don't worry about where they will take you, stop yourself, or attempt to achieve anything. This is likely to be more erratic, more like primary process thinking, with seemingly unconnected and unpredictable switches of subject and mood. It will probably feel quite jumbled and nonlinear, the way your sleeping dreams appear to be.

The passive styles, by definition, ask you to let go of your control of your mind. For some people, this raises their anxiety enough to interfere with the free flow of associations and images. More structured techniques, such as those that follow, might be more suitable if you're not yet on friendly terms with what your unconscious throws up at you. Of course, if you've been doing dreamwork regularly, the passive forms will seem more familiar and less intimidating.

Techniques at the more passive, less structured end of the continuum are best when you're feeling very stuck or very confused. If you can't brainstorm, come up with a list of 100 solutions, step outside the problem, or think of a number of alternatives, the passive style allows you to let go of objections and rigid thinking that contribute to keeping you stuck. If you have no idea of your direction, what might surface in a vague and muddled way in a passive form of visualization may be the first key to unlocking a series of doors on your path.

## Steps for Passive Creative Visualization

1. Retreat to a place where you will not be disturbed by pets, people, or telephones. Wear earplugs if you think this will help.

2. Get comfortable. Loosen tight clothing, sit cross-legged on a meditation cushion or on a chair with your feet flat on the floor—whatever is most comfortable for you.

3. Close your eyes.

4. Consciously relax your face and your shoulders. Your hands should be loose in your lap.

5. Breathe. Take some deep, comfortable relaxing breaths. Pay attention to the regular, even pace of your breathing. Don't force it to speed up or slow down. Just breathe.

6. As thoughts and images start to rise, allow them to come and go as if they had a mind of their own.

7. Notice what passes through your mind. These thoughts and images are neither right nor wrong. Just notice what comes to mind and the emotions associated with them. If you have very strong emotions or feel uncomfortable, you can open your eyes and return to the world around you. If your anxiety becomes too uncomfortable to sit, stand and stretch and return when you are ready.

8. After about twenty minutes, open your eyes and reflect on what you noticed. (You may want to lengthen the time as you become more experienced.)

9. Do a journal entry about this experience. When writing about it, be sure to include the "raw data" of what passed before your mind as well as your emotional and intellectual reactions.

10. Do this once a day for a week to ten days.

11. What patterns do you notice? What information does this give you about yourself that you didn't have before?

12. What action might this information call for, if any?

## ACTIVE VISUALIZATION

Active styles of creative visualization might follow a script like the one that follows or another that has more appeal for you. It has more structure and conscious control. You might consider writing your own script and having someone else read it to you, or tape-record it to play back to yourself. Shakti Gawain, in *Creative Visualization,* offers several scripts, as do many books on meditation, stress reduction, and other self-help subjects. Alter any of these scripts to suit your personal taste and preferences.

The more active techniques of creative visualization are useful when you have a specific goal and would like to establish its subtle aspects in your unconscious. Doing this helps in achieving these goals. The more detailed you imagine the outcome, the better.

To create this active style of visualization for yourself, decide on your specific goal and map out the order of specific steps to take you there—the strategy. What will it take to achieve your goal? What small, first steps do you have to take?

If I picture myself having a comfortable retirement, feeling secure that my investments and income will meet my needs, then what do I need to know? What do I need to feel more secure? What will my expenses be? How much do I allow for travel? Can I anticipate the rising cost of living? What is my savings plan? How much per month or per year? What, exactly, do I have to do to accomplish that? Does that mean I have to think differently in order to change my spending habits today?

Specifically, the visualization might come down to my seeing myself cooking more instead of eating out three times a week. Maybe I have to break down the steps further into even more specific images that will result in an appropriate savings plan.

---

TONYA, an artist, teacher, and illustrator of children's books, did the following active imagination. Entering a calm and trancelike state, she said to herself, "Show me my bliss."

Tonya describes these scenes as appearing in her mind like a children's picture book.

> I see a little white house. It's mine and I can keep it perfect in every detail because it is so small.
>
> I am baking bread. I see one slice of bread on each of eight plates, each slice spread with homemade butter and jam. I am to serve eight ravens; I am feeding the birds.
>
> I am gardening. Every plant needs something special. I have many plants, very diverse in their requirements, but I know each one individually and I know what it needs.
>
> I walk to the market, carrying a little basket. I buy one of each vegetable—the best, most perfect one for vegetable soup. The combination will make a perfect blend of flavors.
>
> At the end of my day, I climb into my hammock with a bunch of fluffy puppies and we fill the hammock and cuddle as we watch the sun set.

Tonya said these five short scenes were about the different aspects of her life. As a successful artist and teacher, more public than she often wants to be, she often longs for solitude, simplicity, and ordinary pleasures—all of which are contained in this active imagination. The meaning of the individual symbols were clear to Tonya, representing her spirituality, home life, relationships with her husband and friends, and nurturing her students. It reminded her to have no more than she needs, to keep things simple, and not let herself get overloaded.

What reactions did you have to Tonya's active imagination? What do they tell you about yourself?

## Steps for Creative Visualization

1. Decide specifically what you would like to visualize, such as your future home, a satisfying relationship, an emotional state of serenity and peace, or a festive gathering of the people you love.

2. Add as many details as you can, using all five senses, including your body position, lighting, setting, other people who would be present. Add music and applause if it's appropriate.

3. Add the excitement, pleasure, joy, and satisfaction you will feel in these circumstances.

4. Expect the wanted outcome to happen in time.

5. Repeat steps 1–4 frequently.

### GUIDED IMAGERY

Some people use the term *imagery* as a synonym for *visualization*. I think of guided imagery as offering more specifics. The reader or guide may suggest a specific setting or place. The story already has a structure onto which you can place your personal preferences.

Here is an example:

*Take some deep breaths and go inside yourself. Relax the places in your body that feel tense. Smooth out your forehead and breathe. Then imagine yourself in comfortable, loose clothing, including your most comfortable walking shoes, sneakers, or bare feet. With your eyes still closed, imagine stepping outside your front door. When you open your eyes in your imagination, you are pleased to discover rolling green hills before you. The sun is warm on your shoulders, and the sky is very blue with just a few wisps of clouds. Patches of wildflowers are scattered beside the path as you walk and you notice the bees and other insects intently moving on the flowers and making a pleasant hum. There's a comfortable breeze and you know you can walk for as long as you like.*

*You continue strolling, feeling very relaxed and at peace with yourself. There are shade trees as you walk and each one has a bench or lounge chair where you can stop. When you are ready, you choose a place to sit or lie down, gazing at the sky above.*

*In a little while, you see a figure walking toward you. As the figure approaches, you recognize who this is. This is a very wise being and you know you can ask a question or learn what you need to know. Allow that conversation to unfold in your mind.*

*(Silence for ten to fifteen minutes.)*

*The figure bids you well in the way you like best and you walk back the way you came, arriving at your own front door in a few moments.*

Notice that the content has some structure to *guide* the listener toward some specific experiences, but also allows for some personal variation. The question and the dialogue that follows come from the individual, rather than being imposed by the text. As with all of these exercises, the amount of structure is on a continuum of very structured to almost not at all—just observing whatever surfaces in silence.

## WHAT YOU CAN EXPECT

You can expect to be surprised, delighted, even puzzled by what surfaces in any of these exercises. The same way your sleeping dreams puzzle you and seem mysterious, so can the images, words, and emotions of a visualization or guided imagery. Know that your mind is your friend, and your unconscious is a source of wisdom and creative imagination. You may be puzzled, but trusting the process will open you to new vistas and possibilities. Expect the best parts of who you are to surface, even when they are in disguise. Expect the unexpected.

## CREATING A PERSONAL LIBRARY OF IMAGES THAT WORK FOR YOU

One of the many advantages of creative visualization that probably accounts for its popularity is that it gives people a sense of power and control in difficult times. By having images you can call up at will, images that soothe and comfort, you can return to them whenever you need them. Stuck in traffic that isn't moving an inch and no way to get off the expressway? You can go to your private haven in your mind for a few minutes' rest. It's free and it never closes.

## INTERPRETING BIZARRE OR "OFF-TOPIC" IMAGES

In Chapter 6, we saw how incubated dreams might offer an answer that didn't seem like an answer at all. Recall how my question about soul loss brought me a dream of my father murdering my nephew Justin. In the same way, the images or stories that come to us in creative visualization and guided imagery may seem off topic. If you trust that your unconscious understands the question, you can trust that you got an answer. Still stumped? Ask someone who knows you well, as suggested before, for his or her input about these puzzling images. Or incubate a dream for help!

For me, insanity is super sanity. The normal is psychotic.
Normal means lack of imagination, lack of creativity.
—Jean Dubuffet

## TROUBLESHOOTING THE ABSENCE OF IMAGES

If the concepts of fantasy and creative visualization do nothing for you or if you have no images when trying any of the exercises suggested in this chapter, don't worry. Everyone is different and there's nothing wrong with you if no images come. Try the techniques in the other chapters of this book and find one that works for you. You might also discover your own style of inner exploration while experimenting with those offered here.

Find what works for you and then do it!

## Dream Partner for Inner Work

1. Choose someone you think of as an equal.

2. Begin with an understanding that you will both share dreams.

3. Select a person who respects you and your differences.

4. Agree that it is acceptable to disagree.

5. Choose someone you can trust with all your secrets.

6. Have an agreement about confidentiality.

7. Agree that you each have a right to set your own boundaries about sharing memories, dream interpretations, and associations.

8. Be sure your dream partner understands that the dreamer is the final authority on the dream's meaning.

9. Agree to relax the norms of "polite" conversation so that you don't have to watch your language, hold back emotions, or be concerned about being politically correct.

10. Agree to speak of any discomfort or issues you have with each other before proceeding to do dreamwork.

## DREAMS INTO ACTION

1. In a relaxed state, tell yourself you would like to meet with "the person I was supposed to be." Invite this figure into a dialogue with you and ask him or her to tell you how to become that person. Make notes on what you're told, however absurd it seems to you.

2. Use the text of the guided imagery in italics on pages 138–39. Read it into a tape recorder, elaborating as you please. Then play it back and see what experience you get. Each time you do this exercise, it will be different.

3. Compare the various results you get over time.

4. Consider showing the results of these exercises to someone who knows you relatively well. Ask this person what comes to mind when looking at the results of your guided imagery exercises.

    *Note:* Make sure you choose someone whom you trust and who is supportive of your desire to make changes in your life. A dream partner might be a good choice. See page 141 for considerations in choosing a dream partner or ally for inner work.

5. Do Tonya's active imagination exercise, "Show me my bliss." What images do you get and what do you think they mean?

CHAPTER TEN

# Waking Nightmares: Crisis and Trauma

The accident may never be integrated, but it may strengthen the integrity of the soul's form by adding to it perplexity, sensitivity, vulnerability, and scar tissue.
—James Hillman

## WHEN A LIFE EVENT FEELS LIKE A NIGHTMARE

Bad things happen to everybody. How bad these events are or how often we experience them varies, but no one gets through life without feeling hurt and wounded at times. We all have problems. Each of us has had some terrifying, awful, or incomprehensible experience that felt like a nightmare, even as it was happening.

Events that can feel like waking nightmares include (but are not limited to) the following:

- Personal attacks such as a mugging, beating, or rape
- Having one's home burglarized or destroyed

- Being a victim of or witness to a terrorist attack, plane hijacking, or similar event

- Being tortured, kidnapped, or held as a hostage or political prisoner

- Having one's life threatened, especially repeatedly

- Being witness to a murder or witnessing the major injury or torture of another

- Being in an abusive relationship with a spouse or other intimate partner

- Being a survivor of childhood physical and/or sexual abuse, especially at the hands of a trusted person or family member

- Being in war or living in a war zone, especially in childhood

- Losing family members in an accident or fire

- Being told that you or someone very close to you has a major or fatal illness

- Being in an accident, especially one that leaves you permanently disabled

- Experiencing combat, military or gang-related situations

- Experiencing a major betrayal by a loved one, family member, friend, authority figure, or other trusted associate

- Learning that something essential you believed about yourself or the world is false, such as learning that the man you thought was your father is not your biological parent

- Having an emotional or mental breakdown, or someone close to you having one

- Losing a child to an accident, homicide, kidnapping, or illness

- Losing a parent or sibling during childhood

- Experiencing a human-made disaster such as a bombing or building collapse

- Surviving a natural disaster such as a tornado, earthquake, flood, tidal wave, volcanic eruption, or hurricane

- Narrowly escaping a brush with death

Any of these events may be so overwhelming as to seem unreal and nightmarish. When we realize it isn't a dream, we have to cope with the event and survive. Once we begin the process of acceptance and activating our resources, we can begin healing our wounds. Mobilizing our coping strategies can contribute to healing. In fact, we can learn and benefit from tragedy and catastrophe.

As many times as I have heard it, I am always amazed when someone says the tragedy she has lived through was the best thing in life that ever happened. A person with a serious injury might similarly say that the accident was something he wouldn't give up even if he could go back in time.

Why do some people come out of major tragedies strengthened and even seemingly enlightened by them, while others disintegrate in despair and depression? Why do children growing up in the same unstable and dangerous home end up with such different lives? One serves a life sentence for murder, another is on welfare or living on the street, and another works in public service with notable accomplishments. What makes the difference? What makes some people tougher and stronger, while others fall to pieces after one or two small setbacks?

Survivors often have similar traits and make similar choices. By knowing the way resilient people bounce back from life's difficulties, both small and large, we can all deal with our own troubles more effectively.

## BREAKDOWNS*

Tough times sometimes feel devastating. We may feel stretched beyond our limits. We say we can't cope and we might feel frozen or paralyzed for a time.

Such breakdowns are normal in the face of overwhelming demands. Through tragic events, people frequently come to terms with their own vulnerability and limited resources. They may say, "It was beyond my power," or "There's only so much I can do."

When faced with traumas on this level, we give up our grandiosity or our belief in our own immortality. Many have said a breakdown is really a *breakthrough*. By disassembling all our walls, belief systems, and assumptions, we can begin to rebuild on a firmer foundation of realism. A shakeup we think of as a breakdown can help us to reorganize our priorities and have a very different perspective on our lives. We make needed changes and can move in new directions, ready to reclaim our more authentic selves.

When my mother was diagnosed with cancer, I was shocked at the possibility of losing her so soon. In the few years before my mother died, I took a close look at my life and how I was spending it. It propelled me into making some major changes, including leaving my work as a microbiologist—a choice I had wanted to make for a long time, but had been putting off.

People who try to do too much might feel as if they are having a breakdown. Feeling "broken" by overwhelming exhaustion or emotions can signal the need for a change. They can pull back and reevaluate how they spend their time and energy.

For me, learning to say, "I can't do that—it will put me over the top," made me feel more competent and in control of my life. Knowing my limits and saying no mean I know how to best take care of myself—to prevent the feeling of having a breakdown.

---

* I am using the term *breakdown* in the vernacular, not as a clinical term for mental breakdown.

# DEPRESSION

Depression—sometimes thought of as one kind of breakdown—can be a signal that you need to make a change in your life. The heaviness, lethargy, and lack of pleasure associated with depression may be telling you that you have gotten off track. Perhaps the depression is a distress signal that you are not on your path or you are ignoring your calling. Sometimes depression comes to draw you inward, to ask you to go into yourself in silence and solitude to hear your inner voice. At other times, it may be a signal that you have silenced yourself or let others silence you. Rather than seeing depressed feelings as what is wrong, the depression itself may be a sign of something else—the need for change. Going inward into the feelings and hearing their messages can be the first step in getting past depression.

*Of course, if depression is prolonged or debilitating or if you are feeling suicidal, you should seek professional help.*

# SYMPTOMS AS METAPHOR

Any physical or emotional symptom, including depression, may be a signal to you to take back your life. It is difficult to interpret a backache or chronic headaches as a message to make a change—especially if you are in frequent pain. It is like asking a dreamer with a nightmare to see the dream as a gift and to listen for the metaphor upon waking, when gasping for air and trying to calm himself or herself. Likewise, when you're in pain, it isn't easy to step outside of it and wonder whether it is a message. However, symptoms can be as potent as the symbols in your dreams and nightmares. If I'm nauseated, I might ask myself, "What can't I stomach?" "What can't I swallow?" "Who or what is my pain?" "What is the thorn in my side?"

Frequently, symptoms are messages of dis-ease. What makes you uneasy or tells you that you have made a wrong turn on the path of your life? What calls you down another road?

Of course, physical illness isn't always psychological and can have purely physiological origins. But being willing to consider metaphoric meaning can be helpful. By paying close attention to your body and your reactions to adversity, you learn about what needs changing in your life. But in order to effect that change, you need to have perseverance, strength, and resilience.

## RESILIENCE

Resilience means the ability to go through a difficult time or a tragic experience and not be conquered by it, but to come out even better than we were before. It's the ability to spring back or bounce back— but to arrive at a higher level.

> What doesn't kill you makes you strong.
> —Friedrich Nietzsche

When we survive a terrible experience and come to some resolution with the events and their consequences, we are often stronger and have more wisdom than we had before the event. We may be able to tell ourselves that if we survived that trauma, we can survive anything. By overcoming the situation successfully, we may be pleasantly surprised to discover skills and coping mechanisms we didn't know we had. Or perhaps we never had to use these abilities before.

Confidence may actually increase after a bad experience. Learning how to talk to ourselves in the face of adversity keeps us focused and competent and helps us discover we are capable adults.

The ability to cope can seem to be inborn. Some children, from their earliest days, startle less easily. They seem less anxious and fearful, and more adventurous. They adjust to new people and surroundings without a lot of Sturm und Drang; they get over upsets more quickly than others do. Other children cry easily and experience more fears and worries, even when they are fortunate to have loving and stable parents.

However, we all have a range of abilities. Aside from any constitutional tendency toward resilience, everyone who desires to be hardier is capable of learning the skills of resilient people and imitating their more effective coping style. Make note of people you think of as tough or hardy—people who aren't easily discouraged. What do they do and what do they say that you can learn from? Ask them what they say to themselves when they have a setback and copy their style until you develop your own.

Many of the following techniques are used by people who rally in spite of the odds. They thrive in unfavorable circumstances because they make the best of what they have, seek out what they need—in people and other resources—and detach from an unpleasant environment. Their ability to be cheerful and buoyant makes other people notice and like them. Because they show hope and fortitude in the face of disastrous conditions, they attract others to their aid, thereby further reducing future risk factors.

## REFRAMING

One of the most effective ways of dealing with crises and upsets of all kinds is to reframe them—that is, to redefine the experience as something different from your initial interpretation. Your first reaction has its own validity, but there are many ways to see any event. Many philosophers have said that it isn't what happens to you, but what you do with it that makes the difference. People who come to value their experience of an accident or illness as a turning point in their lives are reframing the event. It is not Pollyanna or delusional to reinterpret an event as something other than negative. Resilient people seem to be especially adept at reframing.

We all have heard the expression, "When life gives you lemons, make lemonade." This is one kind of reframe. The common use of the aphorism makes it sound easy. But reframing is a new way to approach interpreting and acting on what happens to us in our lives—what something means and how we make that meaning. Reframing helps us rearrange our experiences and their consequences in new and unaccustomed ways.

For example, you might have a problem at work. You have heard a rumor that your company is downsizing and the workforce will be cut by 20 percent. You go into a panic and imagine not making your rent and car payments. You imagine yourself unemployed and you worry about being homeless and having your car repossessed.

Your co-worker, in the same situation, says, "Good! I've wanted to leave this place for years and never would have done it on my own. Now I have a chance to do something different. This is a great opportunity for me to change my life." Same events. Different story. What stories you construct of your life, the narratives you create, make the difference between seeing yourself as a passive victim or as a mover and shaker in your own life. You can begin to create your own destiny by taking responsibility for what happens to you and being determined to make the best of it.

When people say you construct your own reality, most of them are not saying that some objective, external reality "out there" doesn't exist. When a hurricane blows the roof off your house, you didn't just make that experience up in your head or create the weather from your fantasy. However, how you make meaning of it and come to terms with your losses *is* the construction of your own reality. One person is in shock and becomes unable to function normally after losing his house. Another says, "Free at last! All that stuff owned me instead of me owning it. Now I don't have to support all those material things."

Who's right? They both are. Each person makes meaning of the events before him, with the opportunity to frame what happens as a tragedy or a gift. However, to make meaning in the face of suffering is a challenge.

There are two kinds of reframes: *meaning* and *context*. Reframing meaning puts a different spin on the event by attaching a different meaning, as in the preceding examples. Context reframing is becoming aware that behavior in one situation may be undesirable, but those skills are handy and necessary in another situation. For example, I may not like it if someone who works for me questions my decisions on a regular basis and asserts her point of view when I don't ask for it. But when she is negotiating aspects of my business for me with others, I am happy that she has good boundaries, asks lots of questions, and knows how to say no. The context alters my evaluation of what she does. This situation is similar with parents who come to family therapy with a "stubborn, willful" child. They are pleased to be told that their child is less likely to be passive to a child molester or be exploited in some other way later in life. The parents recognize the trait they disliked is admirable and valuable in another context. The story of the Ugly Duckling is a famous context reframe—the duckling was rejected and felt ugly until it was with others of its species and recognized its beauty.

Richard Bandler and John Grinder, in *ReFraming: Neuro-Linguistic Programming and the Transformation of Meaning*, have this to say:

What reframing does is say, "Look, this external thing occurs and it elicits this response in you, so you assume that you know what the meaning is. But if you thought about it this other way, then you would have a different response." Being able to think about things in a variety of ways builds a spectrum of understanding. None of these ways are "really" true, though. They are simply statements about a person's understanding.

In part, maturity is knowing you have choices about the way you think and make meaning, then consciously and with intent, making a choice that serves you well.

## Suggestions for Reframing

1. How do you see the problem? (List five to ten adjectives as part of your description.)

2. What is the opposite evaluation?

3. List five ways the problem is really a blessing in disguise. (Be absurd, if you like.)

4. Assume two of these are true.

5. How does this contribute to your seeing it differently?

6. If this were someone else's problem, what might you say to reassure, comfort, or counsel him or her?

7. Say that to yourself.

8. How might you tell this story differently?

9. Choose someone you admire for his or her excellent problem-solving and coping skills. How would this person deal with the problem?

10. That person is now a role model. What can you emulate?

11. What are the positive functions of this problem?

12. What are the lessons this problem has come to teach you?

13. What issues from the past does this problem bring up for you?

14. How is the impact of your past contributing to your evaluation of this problem today?

15. How is this part of your learning curve?

16. Make up a totally different explanation of this problem. (Tell a new story.)

17. How does retelling your old story contribute to maintaining the problem as a problem?

## SPIRITUAL EMERGENCY

One kind of reframe is to define the difficult circumstances you find yourself in as a spiritual emergency. Stanislav and Christina Grof have collected an excellent assortment of articles in *Spiritual Emergency: When Personal Transformation Becomes a Crisis.* They suggest that many of the experiences that mental health professionals label as pathological can be relabeled as crises of psychological growth and spiritual transformation instead. Hallucinations ordinarily are considered evidence of psychosis, but in other cultures, they are believed to be communications with the Divine. They are encouraged rather than disparaged. Profound grief and withdrawal are thought of as a calling for inner knowing instead of being identified as an isolating depression. Ecstatic, transcendent states following a near-death experience may be evidence of spiritual transformation. After such breakdowns, the person appears changed in a positive way, with a new vitality, awe, and appreciation for everything he or she once took for granted. The experience, with hindsight, reveals itself as a breakthrough to a new state of awareness, often including a calmer and more serene state of being. Some take a giant step toward enjoying life with a sense of purpose and meaning they never had before.

Having some spiritual aspect to your life seems to be one more antidote to succumbing to bitterness and victimhood. Perhaps it is easier for those with a spiritual belief system to make meaning of events and to see beyond the materiality of bodies and possessions into something more. One does not have to believe in a god or ascribe to any particular system of belief to have a spiritual life. Many people have their own spirituality that brings them into a transcendent experience through being in nature, serving others, or some other focus that lends meaning to their lives. Becoming aware of your own spirituality, however you define it, is one more way to deal with life's lemons.

## MAKING MEANING OF TRAGEDY

One method of making alternative meaning of a tragedy is to disconnect from the tragedy to see it as something separate from who you are. Psychologically, we say you dis-identify or disassociate from it, stepping outside the experience to see it more objectively. If I lose my job, I don't have to see it as the end of who I am or as a loss of my identity. I am not my job. It's something I do to make money. I may like my work or get satisfaction from it, but *it's not who I am.*

Of course, some events hit closer to our hearts than others. But one way we can cope is to make meaning of them. Candy Lightner, who lost her child to a drunk driver started Mothers Against Drunk Drivers (MADD). Her activism, fueled by her rage and grief at the senseless loss of her child, substantially changed the way we think about drinking and driving. She contributed to changing the laws in many states and making people more aware of their responsibility to be sober behind the wheel. The Adam Walsh case, and the media attention his father brought to it, provoked changes in the way the police handle cases of missing children.

Sometimes, a very painful incident in your life can be the beginning of your life's mission. Anger at some injustice has been the motivating force behind action—an action big enough to enlighten other people's thinking. At one time, slavery, spouse abuse, and spanking children were accepted by our culture. (The last is still accepted by some.) It takes individuals of passion and daring to awaken the general populace and change norms.

Another way to make meaning of a personal disaster is to see it as a lesson: "I learned a lot from that from that event that I never would have learned otherwise. It took a major illness (accident, loss, and so on) to shake me up enough to see what's important *to me.*"

Frequently, people label their lesson as a wake-up call. A heart attack can *loudly* tell you to stop smoking and start exercising. The death of someone close to you and who is your age might make you see clearly that life is short. It might cause you to finally change your job for one that pays less but is more satisfying and meaningful.

If you have been through a waking nightmare, how was it a wake-up call for you? What did you learn?

## THE VICTIM TRAP

The opposite of being a resilient survivor is falling into the victim trap. When something bad happens, victims blame others and say they have bad luck. They stay focused on the negative event and are unable to move on. They can't integrate it as meaningful in any way or learn anything valuable that might strengthen their character. They take it personally and may see themselves as being unjustly punished. At the extreme, paranoia may set in and they may see others as being out to get them. They interpret even neutral behavior of others as acts of malice or directed at them specifically.

Some victims allow the event to paralyze them. They stay numb instead of finding and processing new ways to cope with whatever they face. They say they can't cope, can't work anymore. Being a victim has its payoffs. By staying immersed in the victim role, they can declare themselves helpless and then expect others to take care of them. They abdicate the responsibility of their own lives. If they seek recourse through the courts through lawsuits and financial judgments, they may collect huge sums of money. But they must also remain focused on how their lives are ruined. Because they must demonstrate their wounds or loss in order to claim and prove damages, they will have to continue to see themselves as sick and helpless. If they seek disability payments or worker's compensation, they cannot allow themselves to reframe the event in any way that might be positive. Any reframe would undo the payoffs. So they wallow. They stay stuck.

Victims allow the event to define them. They say, "I am a rape victim." Even if they call themselves rape survivors, the event looms large in the personal narrative of their lives. They accept the evaluations of others, whether diagnoses or insults (which often bear some similarities), taking on the label or category as a permanent part of their identity. "I'm a manic-depressive." "I'm a sufferer of chronic fatigue syndrome." They succumb to multiple diseases and depression, and embrace aging as an excuse to collapse into incapacity. Unfortunately, this often adds to feelings of worthlessness, increasing their depression.

Some therapies actually encourage the victim mentality. When you tell someone, "You'll never get over this," the statement creates an expectation of being stuck or permanently wounded. Such statements can actually slow down a person's recovery from the misfortune. Some still say that wounded people are "damaged goods" or "scarred for life." This is a potentially dangerous philosophy explored by author Stanton Peele in *Diseasing of America*.

By contrast, resilient people acknowledge the unhappy event as significant, even life-changing, but they are not so closely identified by it. "Still me," Christopher Reeve says. They mourn and then they get over it. They transform their anger and regret into helpful lessons. Note that they *do* allow themselves the painful emotions of grief and rage. They don't suppress or deny their feelings. Rather, they feel them fully and then move beyond them.

However, excessive displays of anger can be bad for your health. People who are chronically angry and who continally express that anger instead of learning how to manage, contain, or rechannel it, are at higher risk for early death from strokes, heart attacks, and a variety of other diseases.

## ASKING QUESTIONS

People who rise above difficulties ask questions and generate lots of different kinds of answers. They ask questions of themselves and they ask them of others. In the face of problems, they ask themselves what they can do, what their choices are. They are not inclined to think in black and white. As in reframing, they approach the problem from a number of different angles and try out, at least in their minds, the possible outcomes. They are willing to ask themselves questions even when they realize that the answer may reveal their personal responsibility in the unhappy events or expose a character flaw they would rather not see. They are willing to ask the hard questions:

Did I do anything to create this problem?

What is my role in making this worse than it has to be?

What can I do now to minimize the problem?

How can I turn this problem into an opportunity?

What did I do right in the past that prevented the problem from ever occurring?

In the middle of the crisis, they are able to ask, "What do I have to do to get out of this alive?" Al Siebert's book *The Survivor Personality* offers many inspirational stories to demonstrate this kind of resilience. He says, "When hit by adversity, no matter how unfair it seems, follow the surviving and thriving sequence: Regain emotional balance; adapt and cope with your immediate situation; thrive by learning and making things turn out well; then find the gift. The better you become, the faster you can convert disaster into good fortune."

Another way to turn your waking nightmare into a wake-up call is to ask questions of others. Choose those whose judgment you trust. You might ask:

What do you observe about me during this hard time that I don't know about myself?

What would you have done in my shoes?

What facts did I miss seeing?

Show me an angle on this problem I might never think of on my own.

Of course, support groups, mentors, and role models (discussed next) are ideal candidates for asking these questions. Remember that if you're going to ask these questions, you have to be willing to really listen to the answers. If they seem off base, that's an opportunity to think in new ways. In the end, you always have the choice to use the information—or not—as you see fit. Do what works for you.

## Choosing a Support Group

1. Decide what specific issue(s) you need support to resolve or cope with—for example, grief, anger management, trauma, addiction or substance abuse, a relationship, or a disease or disorder (HIV, OCD, diabetes, and so on).

2. Do you want:

   a. Professional leadership?
   b. A leaderless group?

3. If (a), call hospitals, mental health facilities, universities, and other professionals for referrals. If (b), check the newspaper for support groups, the chamber of commerce, the Yellow Pages, and friends and acquaintances for groups in progress.

4. Attend a meeting and see how you respond.

   a. Do you feel welcome?
   b. Do you feel comfortable?
   c. Do you feel safe?

5. If you feel uncomfortable, sort out whether your discomfort is reasonable or irrational. Is it based on your fear of change or self-disclosure?

6. Do you need more than one meeting to evaluate the group?

7. Can you grow in this group? How?

8. What are your goals?

9. Be ready to move on when you've met your goals.

## MENTORS, ROLE MODELS, AND SUPPORT SYSTEMS

Resilient people accept help. They accept it when it is offered and they seek it out. Children who rise above their unhappy conditions of sick parents, loss, and abuse are often those children who make an attachment with that teacher, relative, or neighbor who offered comfort and encouragement. They look for people who can help them and they ask for help—by either their words or actions. A sensitive adult who sees this child's need may tentatively offer solace and the child *accepts it*. These children may spend more time at the homes of friends whose family life is more stable and safe. They may visit with the favorite aunt or grandparent and ask to spend summer vacations there or even to live there. They recognize the life preserver and they hang on until the danger has passed.

Resilient adults bounce back in part by consciously seeking out mentors, role models, and support groups. They notice people who have the kind of success that embodies their goal. They emulate people who have the traits of persistence, self-discipline, and tenacity. They copy their role model's habits and confidence until they can feel them as their own. In fantasy, they call up their memories of these people in action and then mentally practice doing those successful behaviors.

People who bounce back from tragedy know how to cultivate friends with whom they can talk and interactions where they don't have to hide their real feelings. They have people to whom they can turn to cry or complain. Their friends can offer sensible help in thinking through possible solutions to problems. Resilient people create and maintain a support system. They ask for assistance in sorting out the issues that make up a problem. They nurture themselves by supporting others. They join support groups to deal with a specific tragedy, but then they move on and get back into living their own lives.

Dealing with any major adversity in life, such as those at the start of this chapter, enables some people to develop empathy and compassion. This sensitivity comes from our own experience of hardship, making it possible for us to truthfully say we understand what another person might be going through. These feelings may lead to a desire to share our vulnerability and emotions with others, increasing the level of compassion and support. The feelings may also propel us to make some contribution to others, offering the service of our time, money, and unique talents or knowledge.

Resilient people also learn to nurture and comfort themselves, often doing alone what others do for them: encouraging themselves, soothing their rattled thoughts and feelings.

## Suggestions for Creating a Support System

1. Stay away from people who:
   > Criticize you (in a way that isn't helpful)
   > Find fault
   > Call you a "dreamer" (meaning it as an insult)
   > Tell you why you can't do what you want to do
   > Sabotage you
   > Derail you

2. Notice the people who support, encourage, and listen to you.

3. Reinforce others' behavior by demonstrating your gratitude to them:
   > Thank them
   > Acknowledge their support
   > Send thank-you notes

Return the favor

Offer small thank-you gifts

4. Network with people who share your interests, values, and passions.

5. Join associations, clubs, and groups of people who share your goals.

6. Offer encouragement and support to others.

7. Hang out with positive, upbeat people.

8. Seek out successful people whose lives are in order. Learn from their good habits.

## 10 Ways to Use a Role Model

1. Choose someone you have admired for some time.

2. What traits make this person admirable?

3. What behaviors do you want to model?

4. Ask permission to be present as much as is feasible to observe these behaviors.

5. Ask what your role model says to himself or herself during tough times and hard choices.

6. When you are stuck about what to do or how to respond in a situation, ask yourself what your role model would do and emulate his or her behavior.

7. Copy your role model's behavior at first and trust yourself to find your own style.

8. Modify what you model to do what works for you.

9. Ask for advice and be prepared to judge whether the advice will work for you.

10. Ask questions.

## EXPECTATIONS: HOPE AND VISION

You have probably heard the adage, "You get what you expect." This statement is frequently delivered in a scolding tone, admonishing the person that their negativity draws negative consequences to them—as if yelling at a pessimist is going to turn him into an optimist.

However, the flip side of this coin is that when you expect success, your chances of achieving it increase enormously. When you imagine a positive outcome and imagine it as vividly as possible, you engage the support of your unconscious to direct your behavior to bring it about. Hope is having a vision of a positive outcome. The conviction that success will occur helps you to recognize and seize the opportunities when they present themselves. Hope is not just a wistful feeling. It's being ready to make your dream a reality by taking action.

In the face of disaster, is there any real meaning to it all? James Hillman says,

> Fatalism answers: Everything is in the hands of the gods. Teleological finalism says: It all has a hidden purpose and belongs to your growth. Heroism says: Integrate those shadows to slay them; put disaster behind you and get on with your life. In each of these replies, the accidental dissolves into the larger philosophy of fatalism, finalism, and heroism.

In the end, we make our own meanings in ways that feel most comfortable to each of us individually. Skills for dealing with waking nightmares *can* be learned.

## Traits of People Who Rise Above Difficulty

1. They dis-identify from the tragedy or trauma; they don't let it define them.

2. They do not see themselves as victims.

3. They make meaning out of the event; it gives them a mission or purpose.

4. They extract what they can learn from the event (prevention, self-awareness, and so on).

5. They use their experience to educate others.

6. They have an inner life and/or spiritual practice (meditation, prayer, enjoying nature).

7. They have artistic outlets for their feelings such as writing, painting, drawing, or music.

8. They recognize they are unique, separate individuals.

9. They are able to insulate themselves from a dysfunctional family or organization.

10. They seek out role models.

11. They ask for help from mentors and coaches.

12. They accept help from others when it is offered and they use it effectively.

13. They value higher education and make the necessary sacrifices to stay in school.

14. They are able to envision a hopeful future with dreams realized.

15. They have a plan, strategy, or steps to achieve their hopeful future.

16. They are tenacious and persistent about reaching their goals for ways to be more tenacious.

17. They do not succumb to addictions (food, alcohol, drugs, sex) to numb their feelings.

18. They nurture themselves.

19. They see a tragic event as only one of *many* life experiences, good and bad.

20. They do not let the circumstance define them (I am not my job or career).

21. They see themselves as winners—in the big picture.

22. They have many sources of pleasure and meaning in their lives.

## DREAMS INTO ACTION

1. When you look over the list of traits of resilient people, which one(s) would you like to enhance in your own life? What first step can you take in that direction?

2. Everyone has had some lemons in life. List three of yours.

   a. _____
   b. _____
   c. _____

3. How did these events make you stronger? What did you learn? How did they raise your ability to show empathy and compassion for others?

4. If you have a lemon in your life that still holds some bitterness, what can you do to move toward resolution? List three possible strategies now.

a. _____

b. _____

c. _____

5. List four people in your support system.

6. If you had trouble listing four people in your support system, what can you do *this week* to begin cultivating supportive relationships?

7. What people have been your mentors and role models? As a child? As an adult? (*Hint:* They can be famous people you never met, living or dead.)

8. List five things you want to do before you die.

a. _____

b. _____

c. _____

d. _____

e. _____

9. If you knew you had only six months to live, but would feel well until the very end, what would you do?

10. What is your spiritual belief system? Do you have a spiritual practice? (Doing a random act of kindness or a regular exercise program can be a spiritual practice.)

11. Choose someone whom you would like to emulate now. What traits or skills do you want to copy?

12. The next time you find yourself in a crisis or dilemma, ask yourself what your role model would do or say and try out this new behavior, pretending you are that person.

13. Want to do something new and challenging? Choose someone to mentor you and ask the person whether he or she is willing. List four people who are possible candidates to be your mentor.

a. _____

b. _____

c. _____

d. _____

14. Describe—in writing, for yourself—exactly what kind of help you'd like to have from your mentor.

15. In this chapter, what grabbed your attention the most? Follow this lead as a way to dream back your life.

PART THREE

# Dreaming Your Future

# CHAPTER ELEVEN

# Self-Expression and Self-Talk

Writing is nothing more than a guided dream.
—Jorge Luis Borges

IF both waking and sleeping dreams are our unconscious expressions of what we are unable to express consciously, then we can examine *what* we desire to express as well as *how* we might deliberately express it. When we know what we have to give and desire to give, then we can investigate ways to do it.

People often slip down the muddy slope of depression when they feel unable to express their true thoughts and emotions. Sometimes we feel silenced by others such as family, work associates, or friends. We may feel censored by what we have been taught by religious or political leaders. At other times, we may stifle ourselves, denying our self-expression in what we write or in other creative attempts.

When we are not permitted to express ourselves, we cannot know who we are. Our unconscious may send up dreams and fantasies, but until we can acknowledge them through some form of expression, they may remain mysterious, troubling, or just forgotten. Those parts of ourselves that we do not own and celebrate in the concrete forms of words and action will haunt us with a nagging discontent. They might cause or aggravate a physical illness, as evidenced by the way we speak. We say our jobs are killing us or the television news makes us sick to our stomachs. We may be speaking more truthfully than we realize.

## SOCIALIZED SILENCE

Each of us has been silenced in some way. We grow up believing there are some things we cannot talk about, certain questions we know we shouldn't ask. Some topics are taboo. Some are dangerous. Some parts of you are unacceptable and mustn't be acknowledged. Every family has its own culture and its own rules, partly influenced by ethnicity, religion, and the time in which it exists. Your family may have allowed certain kinds of expression, but not others. Maybe you can't be an artist or an actor. Maybe you're not allowed to be a scholar or an athlete. Some feelings are allowed, but others are forbidden. Maybe you can be sad, but not angry. Or perhaps you *have* those feelings, but you'd better not talk about them. Communicating or expressing strong emotions in words or behavior may be taboo. In some families, you can be exuberant and excited about political views, but not about sensuality or sexuality. Constraints come from a combination of our ethnic and religious backgrounds, the individual personalities of our family members, and the era in which we grow up and live as adults.

I lived in New York until I was twenty-five. My heritage is Sicilian with a lot of Jewish influence. In my family, anger was expressed openly, but more tender feelings such as gentle affection and emotional vulnerability were belittled. Everyone worried a lot and talked about their anxiety and fear—mostly about money and physical safety. However, my adolescent worries and troubles were trivialized by my parents as nonsense. Growing pains. Kid stuff. No one was athletic or played sports in my family; most physical adventure was discouraged. I was not allowed to have a bike. When I took up scuba diving in my thirties, my mother was vocal in her disapproval. Yet, her candid comments about sex, often in public places, embarrassed me as a teenager. All of these constraints and permissions, sometimes unspoken, influenced what I thought I could or couldn't do as an adult, including what went on in the privacy of my body, mind, and heart.

What wasn't allowed in your family? Were you allowed to be un-happy? Pensive? Confused? Were you permitted your fantasies of a successful adulthood, or were you told you would never amount to anything? Some families allow depression, but discourage happiness. "You're laughing now, but you'll be crying soon," the adults say. To boisterous, laughing children in the next room, some adults threaten, "If I have to come in there . . ."

When we can begin to express what was never permitted, we are on the way to connecting with who we really are. When we find ways to express our thoughts and feelings, we discover our true selves. We begin to dream back our lives.

## YOUR STORY

Each of us has a story. The story of your life can be told in many different ways, but only you can tell it your way. Each time you tell it, you add or delete, embellish, consolidate, and abbreviate. The way your history appears to you changes over time. Memories are not static and immutable. Author Elizabeth Loftus's research demonstrates just how malleable memory can be.

What once seemed to be hardship and misery might appear, many years later, like an excellent training ground for skills that have served you well. A parent who was a stickler for precision and cleanliness might have contributed to your success as an outstanding nursing director or quality control supervisor.

Your story can be reframed in many different ways, but first you have to tell it to know who you are—if only to first see clearly what others have said you are. From there, you can change your story, reshape it and give it new meanings. The way you tell a story contributes to your view of yourself, the beliefs you hold about your abilities and your limitations. Your story can maintain the status quo, if you *use* it to keep things the same. You can use your story to stay a victim or to see yourself as someone who triumphs over adversity.

Some therapists say that you can rewrite your history. Richard Bandler and John Grinder use the techniques of neurolinguistic programming with their clients to create entirely fictitious histories—to offer psychotherapy clients a way to get what they needed but didn't have in their formative years. Deena Metzger, in *Writing for Your Life*, tells of a woman who, as an adult, "gave herself" a much-needed supportive and loving aunt during a childhood when she had neglectful parents.

Did you need a mentor when you were growing up? Do you wish you had had someone who told you that you were smart and deserved advanced education? Someone who told you that you would do well? Invent one. Tell yourself the story in enough detail and frequently enough, and it will become your personal truth. Certainly, Bandler, Grinder, Metzger, and Loftus believe you *can* implant false memories. But if you set out to do it *intentionally* with the desire to diminish the negative beliefs and limits that have held you back, you can free yourself to move forward to wherever you want to go.

## FINDING YOUR VOICE: THE POWER OF WORDS

When we say who we are and what we feel and think, we begin to understand ourselves. When we learn to express ourselves in words without censoring, we begin to have a sense of self. If my thoughts, speech, beliefs, feelings, and behaviors are patterned by the needs and demands of others, then I might not ever know who I am. I can't have a sense of self until I can speak my own truth, especially when that truth might be in conflict with the idea others have of me.

To begin to speak our own truth, we begin by listening to the inner messages that come in fleeting thoughts, emotions, fantasies, and dreams. When we can convert these into words through our journals, we begin to find the voice inside us that was silenced.

For some people, the first step toward finding themselves is in therapy. For many, therapy is the first time anyone has ever listened and taken them seriously, the first time anyone has given full consideration, tried to understand, and been respectful—including when the therapist holds a different viewpoint. To have someone listen without interruption and allow you to discover and express your opinions and ideas is more than therapeutic. For those who have never had this kind of respectful attention, it's nothing short of miraculous. No wonder people fall in love with their therapists and priests.

But you don't need a therapist to discover your own voice, your truth, and your self. You can begin with a personal journal, writing what is on your mind without the censorship that's been imposed on you. Even when you can be certain of having your writing absolutely private, being totally open and honest may still be difficult. When we have been censored all our lives, we end up censoring ourselves *to* ourselves. We may have a hard time allowing ourselves to think certain thoughts or feel certain emotions, let alone write them down on paper.

But we can begin to learn to put those jumbled images and emotions into words in our personal journal. For some, finding a personal voice can come through other kinds of writing as well: poetry, essays, letters to the editor and to people in power, letters to people to whom we have yet to speak our truth. It may come out as articles, short stories, or novels, or in dialogue in plays and screenplays where your characters are allowed to fight and disagree.

Certainly, everything you write will not be literature. All great writers know the value of writing as practice and as discovery. But the act of writing, of naming and defining your demons and your bliss, is therapeutic. Some of your writing may be the first seeds of a larger work. Some of it may evolve into a work that can be brought to the world in newspapers, magazines, or books. Much of it will go no further than your journal, but if you are the only one to read your writing, those words have the power to transform your personal world and how you view yourself. As Deena Metzger and others suggest, creativity and self-knowledge are parts of one whole. Each stimulates the other.

Don't be surprised if your inner critic interferes with your writing. The critic may be the voice of a faultfinding family member or teacher that you have internalized. Banish the critic from the room while you're writing. You can always invite it back (if you want to) when you decide it is time for revision and reworking your writing. When you are writing for expression, this judge deserves no place in the room.

What kind of writing calls to you? How can you best find your voice? A tirade in monologue? Poetry? Short stories? What urgings do you feel as you think of writing down your story with the thoughts and feelings of your life? Make a note in your journal now of the first thing that comes to mind that you might like to write. You may want to take a class or choose among the books on journal writing in the bibliography.

What do you least want to write about? What feels too secret, shameful, or embarrassing? Writing about these things will have the most emotional power to release you from past constraints as well as help you to find your voice.

> The writer is a lifelong meaning-maker, upset about something in the world, angry at some injustice, working through personal confusion and uncertainty, dismayed that others have failed to see this or that, trying to connect, trying to speak, needing to create.
>
> —Eric Maisel

## VISUAL ARTS

Some people see the world in pictures or moving images with form, shape, and color. Words may feel inadequate to capture meaning and feeling. Without characterizing these people as right-brained or more emotional, it is important to honor individual preferences and styles of expression. If art calls to you, or if the idea of writing your feelings and thoughts is too intimidating, you might want to try another expressive modality—even if you think you're "not an artist."

This is about expression, remember, not about producing great art that people would pay for. We may be embarrassed by our early attempts at art and therefore hesitate to play with artistic materials. We may be afraid we'll look silly to ourselves or be mocked by others. We may think of it as childish. But we needn't expect great work from our expression in the visual arts any more than we should be concerned about producing prose worthy of awards when we write in our journals.

When you imagine expressing yourself through the visual arts, what springs first to mind? Doodling with pen and ink or charcoal? Drawing with colored pencils and crayons? Paints? Oils, acrylics, or watercolors? What about fabrics and embroidery threads as your palette? Patchwork quilts? Do you think of clay or papier-mâché? What about other kinds of sculpture, such as carving wood, soapstone, or plaster of Paris? Sand sculpture? Do you want to shape and form or cut away? How about mixed media or collage? Maybe you are drawn to taking photographs that express the emotions you cannot say in words.

What kind of visual art would best express what you have held back all your life? What art can you create that you would have been prevented from making as a child? What was silenced in you that you can express through your art? What can your art do for you now?

Think about what this means to you and make some notes to yourself.

> If you hear a voice within saying, "You are not a painter,"
> then by all means, paint . . . and the voice will be silenced.
>
> —Vincent van Gogh

## ACTION AND MOVEMENT

You might find expressing yourself in physical movement easier at first than writing or art, especially if you grew up in a family where action and the body were celebrated. Or perhaps you are a body-centered person in athletics and dance *in opposition to* your family's values.

Certainly, dance is art as well as movement, but we can find self-expression in many other kinds of body movement, from simply stretching your body to feel its rightful place in the world, to dancing your emotions. I know people who scrub and clean to ventilate their anger, and others who wash and dust as a meditation to soothe themselves. Some people like chopping wood or working in the garden as a form of expression, including making an artful arrangement of flowerbeds and shrubbery. Any form of physical work can also be a form of self-expression. Your exercise program can express who you are, too, from doing push-ups to the elegant precision of hatha yoga or ballet. Or you might want to pursue your self-expression through sports or athletic games.

## MUSIC

Music can be another way to express feelings and ideas. We can listen to certain types of music to deepen our mood, focus our attention, or create a feeling we'd like to have. As I write today, I am listening to Thomas Moore's *Music for the Soul* playing on my CD-ROM drive. I like different kinds of music for different kinds of writing or other activities. Music supports what I want to do. I can use it to pep me up or soothe me, to take me away from the whirl of the world or to get me moving *in* the world.

What music are you drawn to and what does it do for you? How can you deliberately use music to support your own style of self-expression? Perhaps certain kinds of classical music remind you of your more lyrical and gentle self.

Writing music, both words and melody, is another way to use the arts to express yourself. You don't have to write anything worthy of a concert at Lincoln Center or a Grammy award. You can compose a tune that clarifies your emotions or your passion for a concept. If words or pictures don't feel like the right media for your personal style of disclosure, music and sound might fit you better. Try singing the songs you love or going back to playing that instrument you played in high school. Try tapping out a rhythm, drumming, or creating other sounds that speak to you. There is such a wide variety of recorded music and sound today. Explore until you find something that appeals to you. To start, you might want to imitate a composer whose music you love.

When I was a young teenager, my older sister was a friend of singer/songwriter Carole King before she became famous. Carole was a young mother, just barely twenty, and she would visit our home with her baby, Louise, setting up the playpen in the living room. While she talked, she was writing something.

"What are you doing?" my mother asked.

Carole held up the pages of handwritten music. "I'm just writing the violin backup for a song," she said.

"In the middle of all this commotion?" my mother shouted.

I sat in awe. She could chat, listen, and take care of her daughter while she wrote music. All at the same time! She could do what seemed to me an unfathomable activity as easily as I can stamp envelopes while I talk on the telephone.

What is it that you or I can do but we don't know it yet?

Imagine what it must be like to be a Mozart or a Beethoven and have music playing inside your head. Maybe you already have that happening to you. Start writing it down. Or tape-record it and hire someone to transcribe it to musical notation. What musical instruments are in your house that you could play now?

## CREATIVITY

All this may sound as if you're being tricked into being "creative." *Creativity* is a word that frightens a lot of people. It feels like a demand to produce something beautiful and exceptional. In a culture that often celebrates modesty, we are afraid to have the audacity to think of ourselves as creative.

In fact, we are all creative all the time. We use creativity to think of ways to avoid doing what we don't want to do, to make excuses for our shortcomings, and to duck out of our responsibilities. Our creativity can be used to manipulate, deceive, waffle, and procrastinate. We may think of creativity as something noble and virtuous. However, it is an aptitude that can be used toward any goal—practical or not. Perhaps if you believed that creativity can be expressed in an infinite variety of ways, you would permit yourself to acknowledge having it.

## SELF-TALK: LISTENING TO YOURSELF

Most of us talk to ourselves all the time. Some of us do it out loud, but most of us have learned to talk to ourselves inside our heads, often carrying on elaborate conversations with our inner opposing parts.

Whether we are aware of it or not, we create our own moods by what we say to ourselves. We can undermine our confidence and competence by calling ourselves names and by highlighting our mistakes and faults. Research shows that we remember our failures more than our successes. We have better recall of all the things we do wrong than those we do right, although we do more things correctly every day. This pattern of thinking clearly has evolutionary advantages for any species: We need to remember our mistakes, because making them again could get us killed.

For modern humans, most of our mistakes fall into the category of minor social blunders and less-than-effective responses. We can learn from them, but most of us have a tendency to beat ourselves up over them, to undermine our feelings of self-worth.

What we say to ourselves all day in the face of ordinary fumbles and flops can make the difference between taking our lives into a better future or remaining stuck in the old ways and the old mental tapes of our childhood. To become aware of what we say to ourselves and how we say it is the first step to changing these messages.

Many of us object to the kind of criticism we received from our families, teachers, former lovers, and friends. We point to them as the villains who hurt us and "didn't give us self-esteem," but we are often the ones who continue to play their messages.

Dreaming back your life means giving yourself a new set of internal messages. This is more than the now-fashionable technique of having a list of affirmations to recite. We have to give ourselves messages we can believe. I'll never be a ballerina no matter how many times I tell myself I am one. But I can tell myself that I can be agile and flexible, that I can manage what life hands me, that I will get through the hard times, that I am able to learn and grow—no matter how old I get. When I'm stumped, I say, "Come on, Joan. You can figure this out." And I do—usually. If I don't, I know I can learn from someone else who can show me how. I tell myself I will find the resources I need to handle my problems and predicaments.

> Affirmation without discipline is the beginning of delusion.
>
> —Jim Rohn

## LEARNED OPTIMISM

Martin Seligman has popularized the concept of *learned optimism* in his excellent book with the same title. While the common wisdom is that people are born either optimistic or pessimistic, this is learned behavior, often modeled by our caretakers. We learn what to say to ourselves by hearing what others say to us and by what they say to themselves when they struggle to accomplish something. By learning self-talk that is positive, we can be more encouraging. We can tell ourselves any story about the events of our lives and we can learn to tell new stories that serve us better than seeing the world as punishing, gloomy, and scary.

## THE THREE P'S OF PESSIMISM

Martin Seligman demonstrates that pessimistic people make self-statements that include the three P's of pessimism. They view the problem as *permanent, pervasive,* and *personal.* When something goes wrong, the pessimist says:

> I will never get it right; it will always be lousy. (permanent)

> I screw up everything. (pervasive)

> It's all my fault. I'm the only one to blame. (personal)

Optimists, by contrast, know that the problem is temporary and will pass, is a separate instance that may be only peculiar to this time, and may have nothing to do with them personally at all.

For example, if I don't get a call back from a friend, I could say that my life is filled with failed relationships, that it will always be like that, and that it's because I'm not lovable. As an optimist, I'm more likely to say that my friend is busy today and will call me back when she can (the problem is temporary instead of permanent) and that her schedule has nothing to with me or my worthiness as a friend. I also have other friends to call. The situation is specific instead of pervasive and I don't take it personally.

Once I learned the three P's, I was surprised at how many people verbalize this kind of negative thinking that leads them into depression and hopelessness on a regular basis. Notice when you do this to yourself and dispute this kind of thinking by telling yourself the truth about your competency, goodness, and intelligence: "I can do this!" "I can handle this."

## SETTING BOUNDARIES

You can't express yourself if you don't know what your boundaries are. That is, if I don't know where you end and I begin, I might confuse your wishes for my own, your feelings for mine. Some people, sometimes referred to as *empaths,* are particularly sensitive to the moods and beliefs of others, taking them on as their own. Others who are gullible or easily suggestible may adopt different ideas and attitudes depending on whom they are with; their convictions change every time they enter a new encounter. "Oh, yes," these amiable people say, "I feel just that way, too. I so agree!" As chronically passive followers, they may never develop the habit of examining their own beliefs and sorting out their own feelings. They haven't learned how to check in with themselves to ask what their true thoughts and feelings are.

If you think you don't have boundaries (and some people say they don't), ask yourself what you would never do—no matter who asked you to do it. Would you torture someone? Would you rob a bank? Would you get on a bus naked? Most of us have boundaries about our bodies, our personal property, and our inner lives—psychological and spiritual. We have some personal code of rules by which we live. For example, we might not tell falsehoods under oath—even if we believe we can get away with it.

When I teach classes, people often say they don't think they have boundaries. But if I tell them that in this class they will have to empty their wallets to share all their cash with the other class members or take off all their clothes, they quickly discover they have boundaries. Of course, there was one woman who reached for her purse—not to leave the room, but to take out her money!

Generally, we object when people intrude even if we have trouble expressing our objection clearly. We may object clumsily by avoiding contact with the people who violate our boundaries. We can protest by procrastinating or not returning phone calls from these people. Or we may allow ourselves to be violated in some way and then blame the other person—not recognizing that we have allowed the violation. We permit others to control us and then we can rage at them for doing it. Or perhaps we just feel sorry for ourselves, sinking into the victim mentality.

Developing basic assertiveness and defining boundaries are key to dreaming back your life. (See the suggested reading for this chapter.)

## SAYING NO

The ability to say no is part of basic assertiveness, but it's worthy of a separate section here. Stephen Covey says that it's easy to say no when you have a bigger yes burning inside you. What is *your* bigger yes? What is it that you want more than what another person is asking you to do? What would you do if you had the time and resources to do it?

Several years ago, I found myself bumping around and not having the kind of focus and direction in my life that I wanted. My writing was stalled and I felt unable to work on the one project that I wanted to undertake: writing a book about understanding dreams and nightmares. I was socializing with friends, doing chores, exchanging E-mail for two or more hours a day, watching the same news over and over again on television, and not feeling as if I were accomplishing anything of value. If someone asked me to do something or join them in an activity, I felt unable to say no because I didn't have what I thought was a good enough reason to refuse—as if not wanting to do something wasn't reason enough.

When I was certain that I wanted to write a book, Covey's statement resounded in my head: *It's easy to say no when you have a bigger yes burning inside you.* I had found my bigger yes! I told acquaintances that I was no longer going out to lunch; I had a book to write. I became more discriminating about how I spent my time and with whom I spent it. This gave me plenty of time to write my book. And it gave me a better sense of my own individuality and sense of self.

If you've been trained to be nice, say yes, and be agreeable, then the idea of saying no to anyone might be hard for you. Did your family call you selfish for having a mind of your own or your own desires? Perhaps you have trouble with saying no only to certain people or under certain circumstances. When I teach this module in my *Dream Back Your Life* seminars, people often discover they are being nice to people they don't even want to have a relationship with. That is, they are unable to say no because they are afraid the other person might not like them anymore. One woman, Kathryn, complained of having a "friend" who was in constant crisis. She would call Kathryn at all hours, saying she needed something or asking Kathryn to pay her electric bill because her service was about to be turned off. The "friend" didn't drive and was always living on the edge of some disaster, expecting Kathryn to rescue her. Kathryn had a full-time job, a husband, and a family, while her "friend" didn't work and lived alone. I asked Kathryn, "What would happen if you didn't do what she asked?"

"She'd probably never speak to me again."

The other seminar participants clapped.

Kathryn looked around the room in wonder.

One person said, "If she gets mad at you, maybe she won't take advantage of you anymore."

"If you don't rescue her, maybe she'll grow up and learn how to run her own life!" another said.

Kathryn agreed. "I don't even want to be friends with her. She's dragging me down."

When Kathryn came back for another class, she said the woman had stopped calling. She'd had to say no only once. Her so-called friend had found someone else to run her errands.

What Kathryn discovered is what many of us find out when we begin to say no. Our reluctance to say no is frequently based on the fear that the other person will evaluate us negatively. She'll think I'm a bad person. She will say I'm selfish. We worry about what she will think of us even when it's someone whose opinion we don't value, even when it's someone we don't like. *We still want her to like us.*

What we discover when we say no is that the other person is only thinking about herself. Once she is certain we mean no, she quickly moves on to someone else who might say yes and give her what she wants.

Because many of us *do* feel guilty saying no, we also feel as if we have to explain our reasoning. We have to justify our choices. However, giving an explanation opens the door to the other person refuting our values.

"You'd rather see your lover than spend the weekend with your mother?"

Yes.

"You'd rather be alone and read a book than go to a party?"

Yes.

"It's more important to you to work on your book than go shopping with a friend?"

Yes! Yes! Yes!

To avoid getting into the habit of explaining yourself, you might want to practice ways of saying no without explanation. Find your own words that feel comfortable to you and develop your own style, including how polite or diplomatic you need to be. In most circumstances, a simple "No, thank you" (repeated as many times as necessary to each rephrased request) is plenty. Here are some alternatives if you need more coaching. Remember to become a broken record when anyone is trying to weasel an explanation from you or wear you down. You need only have one more no than the number of requests they make.

## 16 Ways to Say No with a Smile . . . Without Feeling As If You Have to Explain Yourself

1. No.

2. No, thank you. I'd rather not.

3. Thank you for thinking of me, but I really must decline.

4. I know your asking me is a compliment, but I just have to say no.

5. How nice of you to ask me, but I won't be able to participate (be there, help you out).

6. I'm not the right person to ask.

7. That's not something I do.

8. I just don't do that.

9. That's not for me. I hope you enjoy it.

10. That arrangement doesn't work for me.

11. That's not a good time for me.

12. I have other priorities or commitments.

13. What an interesting idea! I'm sure you'll find someone else who will want to.

14. No. That's a no-no.

15. What don't you understand about the word *no*?

16. No way!


Become a broken record!

---

SOMETIMES, you may hesitate to say no because you want to decline gracefully. Or, you may be uncertain whether you want to say no to the entire request or only some portion of it. If you feel uncertain or at a loss for words, you can always postpone your decision by asking for more information or more time. Practice saying, "I need some time to think about that." Perhaps you are willing to do some modified form of the request such as, "I'll help out for two hours, but not for a whole day." However, you might need some time to figure out what your limits are.


## OBSTACLES: INTERNAL AND EXTERNAL

The obstacles that get in the way of our expressing ourselves (saying no, setting boundaries and limits) also reveal themselves in how we talk to ourselves. When we tell ourselves what keeps us from our goals, we see the barriers as internal, external, or some combination of both.

Whenever you say, "I can't," why can't you? What is standing in the way?

*External barriers* are often seen as the wishes of other people. The following are examples of external barriers:

- My husband or wife would never stand for that.

- My parents would disown me.

- My boss would fire me.

- That would embarrass my children.

- My lover would dump me.

- My friends would think I was crazy.

- My therapist would call it regressive.

- I'd be the laughingstock of . . .

Other external barriers may be limited resources such as time, money, or the right opportunity.

*Internal obstacles* include the following:

- I'm not physically (or mentally or intellectually) able to do that.

- It's too different from my usual habits.

- I can't bear to be a failure or make a mistake.

- I've never done it before.

- I'm not the kind of person who . . . (goes places alone, takes risks, and so on)

- I'm afraid of how I would feel.

In many ways, we put both categories of obstacles in our own way. By allowing others to make decisions for us, we give up our power. As children, we had to succumb to our parents' wishes, but we no longer have to do that as adults. Many of us replay the issues of our family of origin and are likely to choose mates who will step into the role our parents (or other primary caregivers) played: dominating, restrictive, abusive, oppressive, or overly protective. We are drawn to continuing that familiar dynamic. Freud called it the repetition compulsion. By repeating the pattern, we keep all the old obstacles in our way—even as we are trying to fix them and finally get it right! (See books by Harville Hendrix in the bibliography for an illuminating discussion of how we use romantic relationships to try to repair the problems of our family of origin.)

By reframing obstacles, and seeing how we create and contribute to maintaining them, we can make the changes we want to make. For example, if I say I'm too busy taking care of my family to take an exercise class, I might look at how many things I do that I don't have to do and how my perfectionism about doing them eats up more time than is necessary. I thereby contribute to my being too busy to exercise, but I blame others. Chances are, I am doing things for them they would be happy to do without. Or I could say my spouse won't *let* me do something, a familiar statement made by both men and women. If I hear myself implying that I need permission, I can take back my power and choose for myself—as the adult I am.

> Humans respond not to events but to their meanings and
> can read into any event an endless variety of meanings.
> —Jerome Frank

## LOCUS OF CONTROL

When we recognize that the control and destiny of our lives are more within the realm of our personal power than we thought, then we are able to influence the outcome and institute changes as we need them. If we see ourselves as fixed and determined, constituted by genetics alone ("That trait runs in my family"), designed by our astrological signs ("All Geminis are like that"), or limited by gender ("Real men don't cry"), we will feel helpless and a pawn of fate. We will feel stuck.

Seeing my problem *only* as a disease or seeing myself as a victim of the government and social forces puts the power outside of me. If I see the source of problems as outside of myself, two things happen: I do not acknowledge my contribution to the problem and I do not recognize my ability to change the problem.

By definition, I am saying the problem is something that happens to me, rather than seeing myself as at least partly the creator of my problems.

Stephen Covey speaks of our *sphere of influence,* which is another way to talk about locus of control. Having an internal locus of control means we think of ourselves as the source of our happiness or sorrow. Whether our problems are in relationships, work, or finances, we can do what we can to make changes. With each small change, we widen our possibilities. By seeing a bigger picture and having a longer-range plan, we will see we have more choices—which increase and expand all the time. Often, small changes have big effects.

## SPEAKING YOUR TRUTH

One small change (and sometimes the most effective one we can make) is to speak our truth. Speaking our truth means saying what we think and feel clearly and without being defensive. We say it in I-statements (not you-statements), communicating our calm expectation that we will be accepted and acknowledged even if others disagree.

"I'm not comfortable with this" is an I-statement that doesn't defend, demand, or invite disapproval. It's a clear communication of my state.

We can discuss in what ways I'm uncomfortable, but the sentence *honors and acknowledges my feelings.*

Speaking your truth doesn't mean calling people names, telling them what we don't like about them, or using "truth" as an opportunity to be hurtful or to get revenge. The truth is not about starting a fight or being right. It is about taking the opportunity to be real, to be who we are from moment to moment.

## THE PERFECTIONISM TRAP

What holds us back the most from expressing ourselves is often the fear that we won't do it perfectly. A friend of mine is an avid reader of fiction and very talkative. He loves a good story. I asked him once if he ever thought of writing. "Right. Like I'm going to write the great American novel," he said. His statement seemed to say, "If you can't be perfect, you shouldn't do it at all. What if I do something and it's junk? What if I try and I fail?"

Imperfection is part of what it means to be human. All of us, no matter what level of success we achieve, had to make mistakes before we learned enough to be successful. We will continue to have failures in the middle of success. Having to be perfect keeps people from trying anything new or adventurous, particularly in the realm of self-expression. All of life contains risk. Only death is safe. But if we can take risks, we can open ourselves to all of life, including success, joy, and personal fulfillment. I don't have to be perfect. Even confusion offers us an opportunity to learn.

Richard Bandler and John Grinder, in *ReFraming: Neuro-Linguistic Programming and the Transformation of Meaning,* have something interesting to say about confusion. You can substitute the word *mistake* or *failure* for *confusion* in this quote.

Typically, people think that success is good and confusion is bad. In our workshops, we're always telling you that success is the most dangerous human experience because it keeps you from noticing other things and learning other ways of doing things. That also means that any time you fail, there's an unprecedented opportunity for you to learn something that you wouldn't otherwise notice. Confusion is the doorway to reorganizing your perceptions and learning something new. If you were never confused, that would mean that everything that happened to you fit your expectations, your model of the world, perfectly. Life would simply be one boring, repetitive experience after another. Confusion is a signal that something doesn't fit, and that you have a chance to learn something new.

One of the turning points in my own life was reading *The Spirituality of Imperfection* by Ernest Kurtz and Katherine Ketcham. It literally changed my life. I can now do something new at my best ability and not worry about doing it perfectly. I know that I will learn by doing and improve as I go along.

## DREAMS INTO ACTION

1. What do you like to read?

2. Did you ever write a letter to a newspaper or television station? What was it about? Write again about this subject that motivated a letter.

3. Write the letter again from the opposing point of view. What did you learn?

4. What subject would you be afraid to write about?

5. What can't you say even to yourself? How can you find a way to express these feelings that keep you silent?

6. What kind of art do you enjoy most?

7. When you imagine yourself as an artist, which of the expressive arts do you feel most drawn to?

8. Go to an art supply store and wander around. What materials do you feel most drawn to? If money were no object, what would you buy?

9. Buy yourself some art supplies to play with. Keep it simple. Have fun.

10. Consider inviting a friend over to model clay with you.

11. If you were going to take art lessons, what would you choose to learn?

12. Who could be a mentor for the artist in you?

13. Dance your anger. Then dance your joy. Choose music that matches the mood you want to express through dance.

14. Choose a physical activity you wouldn't ordinarily do, such as working in the garden, building something, or an exercise class that's different from what you usually do. Be aware of your body during this activity. How does it feel to move in these new ways?

15. What specific boundaries do you have (physical, sexual, mental, spiritual, personal property)? List as many as you can think of, but list at least twenty.

16. Who violates your boundaries? How?

17. What do you say to yourself when this happens?

18. What do you do to help others violate your boundaries? In what way do you give them your permission?

19. What is your usual outward reaction to a boundary violation?

20. How else might you react? Give alternative responses.

21. List those people who are hard to, say no to and the reason why it's hard for you.

    *Person:*                          *Reason:*

    _____          _____

    _____          _____

    _____          _____

22. Look for an example of your using the three P's of pessimism. When are you most likely to behave in this way?

23. Who puts obstacles in your way? How do they do that? How do you make it easy for them to put obstacles in your way?

24. Play music and see how your body responds. Do you want to dance? Conduct? Tap out the rhythms? Do it.

25. Go to a store that sells electronic keyboards and musical instruments. Ask to try them out. See what draws you.

26. Make an artistic space for yourself in your home. If you feel an objection coming up, override it and make the space anyway.

27. In a journal entry, speak your truth. What do you hear yourself saying that calls you into your future?

28. What do you do that is your version of the perfectionism trap? What can you change today?

# CHAPTER TWELVE

# Finding Your Purpose

Saddle your dreams afore you ride 'em.

—Mary Webb

When a man has learned—and not on paper—how to remain alone with his suffering, how to overcome his longing to flee, then he has little left to learn.

—Albert Camus

EACH of us is unique with our own talents, skills, and view of the world. We each have something to contribute to each other and to the planet.

What is my purpose? Why am I here? What is my destiny? Am I fated or do I have free will? Who chooses my path? Do I have a task that is unique to me, that only I can do while I am on the planet? Do I have a specific vocation? If I do, what is it?

This book has asked you to make friends with your own mind by noticing what you are saying to yourself in your dreams, fantasies, obsessions, frequent complaints, and reveries. All of these tell you how to hear the chatter in your own mind as important information. That mental noise is asking you to take action in your life. Each piece of information points to your purpose. In each elusive fragment of thought, you are telling yourself what you must do to fulfill your purpose.

What have you learned about yourself in reading this far that points to your purpose? In a short paragraph, make some notes on your present conclusions, however tentative they may seem. If you prefer, make a quick list of 100 things you've learned about yourself. Remember that when making a list of a hundred, it is best to do it all in one sitting, as quickly as possible. It's okay to repeat items that come to mind persistently. Repetition may be a signal pointing you to your purpose. It is pressing to be heard!

If you haven't done the "Dreams into Action" exercises and experiments yet, you might want to go back and do a few that most appeal to you. Just noticing what exercises you like will tell you something about yourself as well. If none appeal, make up variations on some of them.

Perhaps you have done the exercises and you still don't know what your purpose is. This chapter, with a heavier emphasis on exercises and questions for the reader, explores other avenues for finding your purpose.

> Learn to get in touch with silence within yourself and
> know that everything in life has a purpose.
> —Elisabeth Kübler-Ross

## SOLITUDE AND SILENCE

To know our purpose is to hear our calling. Unfortunately, the inner voice is often drowned out by the sounds and demands of our environment. Our family, work, pets, homes, and cars make demands on our time. Radio, television, and print media bombard us with messages about what we should want and how we should feel. They all take us away from our inner knowing of our personal destinies. We have to be still and quiet enough to hear our true calling.

In many societies, it was common practice for people to go on retreat and withdraw from their daily concerns, to be alone and quiet, and to think or pray. In others, a vision quest provided a physical and spiritual testing ground. Silence and solitude were honored as necessary for rejuvenation, restoration, and a renewed communion with the gods or the divine within. It was acceptable to leave one's work and family obligations to go away for days or even weeks at a time. Certain societies had retreats of one kind or another built into the social structure. When men went off to hunt and didn't return until they had meat for the tribe, they had time to be away, mostly silent, and sometimes alone. Societies where women were isolated while they were menstruating provided time for women to retreat from their social lives. In other time periods, people who were drawn to silence and solitude could join a monastery or a convent. In other societies, more solitary people might choose to live on the outskirts of the tribe or community.

In our modern world, going on a retreat is often not as socially acceptable. Today's vacation from work is sometimes more stimulating and stressful than our daily routines. We come back saying we need a vacation from our vacation.

But we can find a few minutes of retreat time each day and a larger block of time if we choose. In daily lives, this means finding a space where we can be alone and be quiet. For some, this is their twenty minutes of meditation. For others, it's prayer or a walk. Most important in planning retreat time—no matter how long it is or where it takes place—is to spend it alone and without the intrusions of other demands on our attention. When you find yourself in solitude and silence, what rises to the surface? What do you discover? If entering this receptive state is anxiety-provoking for you, what might you be afraid to discover?

Consider incubating a dream with a question about your purpose.

> *Higher self and dream maker:*
> *I am ready to fulfill my destiny. Show me the way!*

Don't be surprised if your answer to such a grand question is something that seems quite ordinary.

Expect an answer.

*Expect the unexpected.*

## RITUAL AND YOUR QUEST

Consider creating a ritual to find your purpose.

Humans have used rituals for at least as long as we have recorded the events of our lives. The long-lived practices of blowing out birthday candles, carving Thanksgiving turkeys, and throwing graduation caps in the air show us the pervasiveness of ritual—outside of organized religion. These rituals lend meaning and comfort to our lives. Rituals provide us with a way to affirm what may feel uncertain or unclear. They help us to concretize our beliefs and take the next step into our future.

Starhawk, author of *The Spiral Dance,* says, "Ritual affirms the value of any transition. When we celebrate life changes together, we create strong bonds of intimacy and trust that can generate new culture. When we undergo a change uncelebrated and unmarked, that transition is devalued, rendered invisible."

When we think back on our most emotional memories, they are often attached to rituals, whether secular or religious. By using a combination of language, sound, visual images, scent, and movement, rituals speak powerfully to our unconscious. The ceremony makes real the commitment or the shift in our sense of self.

Some everyday rituals are having morning coffee, giving hugs to say hello and good-bye, saying good morning, and shaking hands. When someone doesn't participate in a ritual we expect him or her to honor, we might feel affronted or bewildered.

You can create your own personal ritual for any reason. Some occasions for ritual might be the following:

- To complete grieving

- To let go or release (a relationship, a hurt)

- To acknowledge a life passage (divorce, empty nest, menopause, going back to school)

- To embark on a new project or life path

- To enhance health

- To make a commitment (to yourself or someone else)

- To ask for wisdom

- To honor or validate a part of yourself

- To take on a new self-image

- To activate your higher self

- To celebrate a success or achievement

- To forgive yourself or another

- To transform anger into action for change

Author Michael Ventura, in *Letters at 3 A.M.: Reports on Endarkenment*, says that ritual is enacting the metaphor. "You get an image, and instead of thinking about it or writing it down or forgetting it, you *do* it. Enact it. Put yourself through the metaphor that the imagination offers. With a little help from your friends." Later, he says, "Ritual unleashes enormous energy."

Because all rituals—religious, sexual, or political—speak to our unconscious, we are deeply affected by them even when we don't share the belief system they express. To be a witness to another's ritual or to observe a ceremony meaningful to another culture is to be touched. Even the impulse to disrupt or laugh betrays how much we are moved by the rite before us. We may *call* it nonsense, but at some deeper level of consciousness, our hearts are pierced, whether or not we want it so. We may joke about a ritual to discharge our discomfort. Or we may dream about it.

If you are still at a loss about your purpose, you might consider enacting a ritual using the following steps. Feel free to add what feels right to you, especially in terms of specific symbols that speak to you personally.

## 10 Steps to Design Your Ritual

1. Define the purpose or outcome ("I want to let go of my anger at my ex").

2. Create the opening (a statement of your intent).

3. Set the scene (place, furniture, altars).

4. Choose materials and tools (candles, incense, music, drums).

5. Engage the five senses (vision, sound, smell, taste, touch).

6. Use symbols with personal meaning.

7. Use body movement or gesture.

8. Choose a witness or audience.

9. Enact the ritual.

10. Close with words to affirm your intention (closing prayer, poem, announcement, affirmation).

---

THE combined strength and comfort of personal ritual became clear to me when I decided to do one for myself. After several years of trying to contact my older sister and only sibling, I knew I had to let her go. Five years of writing her cards and notes for birthdays and holidays with no response made it evident that she didn't want to hear from me. When she finally answered my last letter of love and apology for all my unknown trespasses, she wrote back to tell me not to contact her again. She said that if I truly wished her peace, I'd leave her alone and not answer her letter.

After the initial shock and grief, I took her at her word. I couldn't understand it, but I knew I had to respect her decision. Though she had disconnected from most of the family, it was little consolation to tell myself I shouldn't take it personally. So I designed a simple ritual to let my sister go so that I could move into other close relationships. I asked a friend to be a witness.

The summer I was eight and my sister was fourteen, my sister went away to Girl Scout camp for two weeks. She was my buffer and solace in the crazy household where we grew up; we shared a small bedroom until she got married. When she returned from what seemed like an endless two weeks, she brought me a small birchbark canoe as a gift. I saved this as one of my precious treasures for nearly forty years. For my ceremony, I decided to burn it, along with two photos of us together, one with my mother also. Outside, with my friend next to me, I knelt in front of a bowl and lit the photos and the canoe. My friend was silent without my having to ask her to be. I said aloud, "Camille, I release you. You don't want to hear from me. As you requested, I will leave you alone. With this smoke, I release you to the universe. I will honor your wishes and I will not contact you. If you want me, you know where I am." I watched the photos and the canoe burn.

I expected to weep, but didn't. For a few moments, I sat there, surprised to find I felt lighter. I knew I had done all I could. I no longer felt angry. I felt some sadness, but I also felt more at peace. I could let go of wondering what I did wrong. With the ritual, I made peace with her in my own mind, without having to win her back. I could stop wondering what it would take for her to want to be part of our family again. I took a deep breath.

In the days that followed, I told this story to my closest friend, Joyce. When she next visited me she handed me a small, ribboned package that held a crystal canoe.

She said, "I want to be your sister . . . and this canoe doesn't burn."

---

RITUAL helps us to provide the space for change and to make a concrete ceremony to enter the change. It allows us to let go of the old and begin anew. As old as humankind, rituals make the ordinary and the secular into a sacred transcendent moment.

## DEFINING YOUR PURPOSE

Your purpose is not simply a goal or a desire to have something. Goals and desires are vehicles to help you realize your purpose, but they are not your purpose. Goals are part of the strategies that we'll look at in the next chapter.

Your purpose is who you are at the deepest level of your being, your sense of why you are here, a calling to your personal fulfillment and the realization of your Self. You may glimpse your purpose in peak experiences described by Abraham Maslow when you feel that you are connected to all around you in a meaningful or satisfying way. A peak experience may be among those times when you felt totally content, when your life and circumstances seemed suddenly perfect, and when you felt love for everyone and everything around you. What was different about those times? What pattern do you notice?

You may also get a glimpse of your purpose when you experience *flow,* as described by author Mihaly Csikszentmihalyi. When you are in flow, you lose yourself in a task that is both challenging and satisfying at once, forgetting all sense of time, unaware of any separateness from what you're doing. The descriptions of this state are very similar, whether from athletes, artists, musicians, writers, cooks, or teachers. What do you do that you love so much and become so absorbed in that you lose track of time and feel so immersed in the task that you can't be distracted easily? Are you ever so absorbed that you don't even hear your name being called?

Some of us have had these experiences at some point in our lives and we look back on them with nostalgia and longing. However, we don't go back to the activity or interest that created them. We feel a kind of homesickness for those good old times, but we do nothing to recreate or continue those old pleasures that were once so satisfying. What activities or interests trigger this feeling for you?

Your passions are also signs of your purpose. What gets you really excited and "juiced" is something of great meaning to you. If you feel passionately about something and would change it if you could, you have a sense of purpose in front of you. What is meaningful to you, especially what is meaningful enough to light your fire and propel you to action, is a sign of your purpose.

Consider how some people have defined their purpose:

- I am here to add happiness to the world by being kind to others.

- My purpose is to share my love of reading with children and improve literacy worldwide.

- My calling is to spread God's word and God's love.

- I'm on the planet to provide a safe, loving, and encouraging environment for all of my family to grow to their full potential.

- I have always felt I was here to teach others to respect Mother Earth. Geologically. Not just the living parts.

- My life's work is about teaching self-acceptance to as many people as I can.

- I am an instrument of peace and service.

- I am here to learn. Everyone and everything are my teachers.

Stop now and write a few sentences about your purpose as it concerns different areas of your life—personal, professional, and spiritual. Remember that it is always changing and evolving—you might write it differently tomorrow. You might want to consider writing a paragraph every day as part of your journal entry as you explore your purpose.

> Nothing contributes so much to tranquilizing the mind
> as a steady purpose—a point on which the soul may fix
> its intellectual eye.
>
> —Mary Wollstonecraft Shelley

Once you are clear on what your purpose is, you may want to do a ritual or an additional ritual to affirm your purpose. Think of this kind of ritual as clarification of your intention and a repetition of your vows to yourself. Rituals of renewal strengthen your sense of purpose as you waver along the way.

> Everyone longs to be special, to be a center of importance
> and value, to possess life's fullness even unto immortality,
> and everyone spends energy in pursuit of those things
> that, according to his own level of understanding, will
> fulfill these longings.
>
> —Philip Novak

## EXPLORING YOUR GIFTS

Each of us has come into the world with certain gifts. These special talents and aptitudes may be pointers to our purpose. Make a list of at least 100 of your gifts and talents now. Don't be modest. In fact, forget anything you ever learned about humility and modesty for this exercise. You may even be good at things that you don't think of as special talents, but have something hidden in their meaning that when reframed may point to your purpose.

For instance, if you can work in a messy environment without having to get up and clean everything first, without having it all perfectly ordered, you might have labeled yourself sloppy. The reframe is that you can ignore the mess and have the ability to stay motivated and focused in spite of what might be terribly distracting for someone else. That could mean that you could flourish in an environment that other people would find impossible to work in. Or that you have great powers of concentration and motivation that are not easily undermined by chaos. That's a hidden talent. List the talents you know are talents such as *attention to detail* or *organizational skills* and then list the ones that may be hidden by the label "bad habits," such as not worrying about things that others are concerned about.

Again, *don't be shy and don't be modest.* You can decide how much you want to shine after you peel off that first layer of humbleness. This is a personal exercise that you needn't share with others unless you choose to.

> Most of us simply do not live full-time within a single moral structure that gives us a set of instructions on how to be, or even a good clear set of guidelines on how to figure it out for ourselves. Nor do we, as individuals, have ironclad "characters" with solid personal ethical codes that apply wherever we go. We just don't have, most of us, what you could call a clear moral identity any more than we have an enduring psychological one.
>
> —Walter Truett Anderson

## POINTERS TO YOUR SPECIAL SKILLS AND TALENTS

If you had trouble with the previous section, you might think about the times in your life when you learned something surprisingly quickly. Perhaps you had to be shown something only once and you got it right away, while others needed several explanations. When did you find something really easy? Maybe the way computers work just made sense to you, and working with them was as comfortable for you the first time as if you'd been doing it for thirty years. Maybe it was the first time you planned a garden, wrote a grant, prepared a lesson plan, changed a recipe, or organized a party. Doing this task, even as a complete novice, you discovered you already had most of the skills; you could even anticipate and avoid mistakes before you made them.

Going back as far as you can in your memory, make a list of the times you learned something easily and quickly. Try to cover each aspect of your life growing up, including the following:

- Physical tasks (such as using special equipment and building things)

- Athletics (such as running or hockey)

- Mental challenges (such as your first encounter with geometry and algebra, or memorizing a script)

- Interpersonal skills (such as knowing how to read other people's moods and reactions, or being able to understand what others are trying to say and helping them by reflecting what you hear)

- Music (such as being able to play a song on the piano after hearing it only once, being able to play an instrument you've never seen before, or singing without formal training)

- Dance (such as seeing dance in your mind when you hear something described or learning steps easily)

- Language (such as being able to identify and imitate accents and dialects, learn foreign languages easily, or write coherently with little assistance or struggle)

- Fashion and style (such as making or designing your own clothing as a young child)

- Cooking and baking at an early age (perhaps without recipes or with very little instruction)

- Mechanical know-how (such as knowing how to fix things, or being eager to take equipment and tools apart and put them back together)

- Emotional intelligence (such as being able to manage your feelings and make good judgments, being wise and mature for one's years, or being cool in a crisis)

- Logic and judgment (such as being able to sort through and articulate the main issues when everyone else is stuck in minutiae)

- Math skills and money management

- Decorating

- Love of nature (such as the ability to recognize and identify plants, bird calls, or animal behavior)

These are only a few of the possibilities of your special skills and talents that may have surfaced early on and then were put aside while you were being "practical and responsible." What special talents are yours?

> No loss by flood and lightning, no destruction of cities
> and temples by hostile forces of nature, has deprived man
> of so many noble lives and impulses as those which his
> intolerance has destroyed.
>
> —Helen Keller

## MAKING MEANING OF YOUR LIFE

Purpose and meaning are mirror images of one concept. When what we do lends meaning to our lives, we have a sense of purpose. *Our purpose is what gives meaning to our lives.* When we spend our time doing work that feels meaningless—or worse, work that feels destructive to ourselves and others—we become depressed and irritable. We go on automatic, trudging through our days with the feeling that our lives are being spent without an important purpose. We long for something more, but we feel stuck. Whatever we do, we have the ability to assign it meaning or not.

Sometimes, the routine aspects of our responsibilities obscure our purpose. The repetitive tasks of any job can easily make us forget the larger scheme of our task. Doing laundry and making meals is part of the larger job of providing a home for family members to grow in. Doing paperwork and filing are part of caring for patients in a hospital. You can say, "I just do secretarial work," or "I am part of the record keeping in a hospital that takes good care of people."

## DISCOVERY BY THE VIA NEGATIVA

Another way to discover your purpose and meaning is to examine what you don't want. This is sometimes called making a decision by process of elimination. What you rule *out* can help define what you want *in* your life.

What feels wrong in your life? What is unacceptable to you in your work? What do you do that goes against your grain?

Consider these examples:

- Hating to get dressed up in the kind of clothing you're expected to wear at certain occasions (such as a business suit, makeup, or jewelry)

- Feeling confined by working indoors, especially in an office building

- Recognizing that your daily work and responsibilities leave you no time for creativity, individuality, or innovation (you do the same things day after day without learning or being challenged)

- Finding yourself buying things you don't want because you believe you have to show others a certain level of material success

- Living in an environment that feels unnatural to you (for example, a city mouse in the country or vice versa)

- Spending time with people whose company you don't enjoy

- Engaging in activities that are not or are no longer pleasurable to you

- Feeling that you are living a life someone else designed for you

- Keeping hours or a schedule that doesn't match your own circadian rhythm (for example, trying to be a night person when you're a morning person or vice versa)

- Attending meetings or other gatherings that seem like a waste of time or counterproductive to the purported aim

- Feeling that your life is unnecessarily complex

As you read this list, you may have thought of the things you do or ways in which you now live that go against your grain. List as many of those as you can think of now. Notice how often you feel you are out of sync with your truest self. Add to your list whenever the feeling arises.

Knowing what you *don't* like can help you discover what you *do* want in your life. Your patterns of withdrawal and escape or even the *desire* to escape can be an indicator of your true purpose. When do you have that feeling? What are you saying to yourself that helps create this feeling? What do you want to run *from*? What do you want to run *toward*?

The resolution of what we don't like in our lives can be the beginning of dreaming back our lives. Whether we decide to simplify, change our residence, or revamp our personal situations entirely, we are saying no to one thing so that we can say yes to something else.

## VALUES

Sometimes a fanciful question can help us clarify our values. What are your values? What is most important to you? One of the exercises in Chapter 8 asked you what you would do if you won the lottery. The fantasy of complete financial freedom offers a window on what you treasure most.

To clarify the things you want in your life, make a list of your values. Common values include the following:

- Health
- Importance of having a partner/spouse/mate
- Honesty
- Kindness
- Loyalty
- Generosity
- Respect
- Love
- Intimacy
- Children
- Solitude
- Family connections
- Intellectual growth or education
- Pleasure
- Security
- Freedom
- Peace
- Justice
- Ambition
- Authenticity
- Cleanliness
- Order and organization
- Responsibility
- Work satisfaction
- Creativity
- Self-expression
- Care of the planet
- Rights of all people
- Animal rights and the rights of other living beings
- Spirituality or religion

These are only some possible values. Add your own, including specific examples under any of these categories. Valuing freedom can mean many different things to different people. Freedom *from* something (violence, fear, oppression)? Freedom *to do* something (vote, travel, express yourself)? In your own list of values, be as clear and specific as possible. Defining your values will help clarify your purpose and how you achieve it.

When we know what our values are, we can live by them, making choices in how we spend our time and other resources that are based on our core values. Frequently, values come in conflict with one another. I can value both solitude and intimacy, but will have to choose one over the other at certain times. In *The Notebooks of Lazarus Long*, science fiction author Robert A. Heinlein said, "You can have peace or you can have freedom. Don't ever count on having both at once."

Conflicting values call for balance and proportion. Both elements are needed to dream back your life. When we are immersed in living by one value, another one may seem to be overshadowed. The needs of family members or a desire to finish an important project may keep you from tending to your other values, such as cultivating your primary relationship or advancing your intellectual growth.

While I was caring for my mother when she was dying, my own personal life was neglected for at least a year. I withdrew from the world and didn't see friends. After my mother's death, I had an opportunity to make some changes in my life. I reentered the world with a different perspective and new values that were reflected in the changes I made. These included adding meditation and an exercise program of yoga, giving up alcohol, and taking my writing and my study of the craft of writing more seriously. I also chose my friends with more care because I understood the importance of having deep connections.

Rushworth M. Kidder, in his excellent book *How Good People Make Tough Choices*, advises us that living by one's values isn't always easy. "Those who live in close proximity to their basic values are apt to agonize over choices that other people, drifting over the surface of their lives, might never even see as problems. Sound values raise tough choices; and tough choices are never easy."

Expect that your values will change over time. At different life stages, we emphasize different values. Some values may temporarily take a backseat.

## SPIRITUAL COMPONENTS: COMPASSION, SERVICE, ACCEPTANCE

> Spiritual growth is no more than expanding personal con-
> sciousness upward from the present stage of development
> toward the next higher level. For most of us, this means
> mastering the ego-based strivings of early adulthood,
> then clearing away impediments against opening the
> compassionate heart.
>
> —John E. Nelson

People who have a sense of purpose and meaning in their lives usually have what I think of as a spiritual component to their purpose. Self-actualized individuals, by definition, have entered what is sometimes called the transpersonal dimension. I am not suggesting that they have a metaphysical belief system or accept any kind of spirit world, though they may. If you ever heard Carl Sagan speak or have read his books, you would know that he was deeply moved by the natural world. Sagan's love of science and the quest for scientific knowledge and understanding was more than scientific. His awe, appreciation, and desire to share the pleasures of his fascination with the cosmos and its laws had deeply spiritual qualities, although he was not a believer in any religious doctrine.

We can enter what might be thought of as a spiritual domain by considering how we treat others and ourselves. Many people define a calling in terms of their compassion for and service to others. Our most meaningful experiences may be when we offer some assistance and comfort or help others in some way. We may discover we feel most satisfied with ourselves when we are being generous and available emotionally to someone in need, when we are not thinking of ourselves alone. By volunteering our time and efforts to those causes that touch our hearts, we find meaning and purpose; we begin to enter the transpersonal dimension.

This concept can be misinterpreted as a contradiction of all my previous statements about carving out time for yourself and listening to your own aspirations and callings. But when you can truly be who you are and take care of yourself, you can give to others. *You must* have *a self to give of yourself.* You know what you have to give and you know how to fill yourself up to give again. This gives you the serenity and inner peace that it takes to be compassionate and accepting of others who are different from you. Compassion is more than empathy or toleration of others. It means remembering that we are all made of the same stuff. It means we want to relieve the suffering of others.

Abraham Maslow said that self-actualized persons are also the most compassionate. They are the people who get out in the world and fight injustice and intolerance. He says that "to become a better 'helper' is to become a better person. But one necessary aspect of becoming a better person is via helping other people. So one must and can do both simultaneously."

Author John Welwood, in *Paths Beyond Ego,* edited by Roger Walsh and Frances Vaughan, agrees:

All the great spiritual traditions teach that single-minded pursuit of one's own happiness cannot lead to true satisfaction, for personal desires multiply endlessly, forever creating new dissatisfaction. Real happiness, which no one can ever take away, comes from breaking our heart open, feeling it radiating toward the world around us, and rejoicing in the well-being of others. Cherishing the growth of those we love exercises the larger capacities of our being and helps us ripen. Since their unfolding calls on us to develop all our finest qualities, we know that we are being fully used. Thus all the current difficulties of relationships present us with a rare opportunity: to discover love as a sacred path, which calls on us to cultivate the fullness and depth of who we are.

## SPIRITUALITY VERSUS RELIGION

The spirituality that underlies many of the practices in this book is not part of any particular religion. You do not have to believe in any god or any organized system of beliefs. Nor do you have to be a non-believer. Finding your own spiritual style—even if it simply means believing in your higher self—is up to you.

After doing the exercises and experiments in this book, you might discover that a particular religious belief system, perhaps the one you were first exposed to or one new to you, calls you to service. You might just as easily want to find your purpose through more secular means, which can also offer spiritual rewards.

## CURB YOUR DOGMA

When we discover what gives our life meaning, when we are excited about the answers we've found, and feel happy to have found a path that satisfies, we want to share it. The temptation is to tell others about how wonderful our solution is, how *they* can do this, too, how they can also find this happiness. We forget that what has been the right combination of actions for us is unlikely to be the same for anyone else. Like us, they have to explore, listen to their desires and callings, and discover what is right for them. Imposing our own views on them—whether spiritual, artistic, or social—is a violation of their individuality. We didn't like it when others told us what was right and what we should do, and they won't like it if we do it to them.

Certainly, in my own overflowing enthusiasm about my life choices, I have made this mistake—more times than I'd like to admit. Even as I prepared to write this book, I wanted to be sure that I would offer a variety of methods to dream back your life—*your own life*, not mine. I know how easy it is to be dogmatic.

The inclination to evangelize is a natural part of our enthusiasm when we have a personal revelation of truth. But we must remember that it is *personal and individual* if we want to be a model for others. At the same time, we must hold onto "beginner's mind" so we do not become stuck in the traps of our own self-imposed dogma.

## DREAMS INTO ACTION

1. Do you have trouble spending time alone? If the answer is yes, write in your journal about how it feels and what it means to you to be alone.

2. Do you make a distinction between being alone and being lonely?

3. What do you do to have solitude in your life?

4. When do you have quiet times? Think of ways you can surround yourself with silence so that you can hear your inner calling.

5. What makes you angry or outraged? What do you see as injustice?

6. How do these strong feelings point to your purpose?

7. What is your purpose? Write your purpose in one or two sentences if you haven't already done so.

8. What are you passionate about? Any activism? What cause would motivate you enough to write a letter or join in a march or demonstration? Write about these issues in your journal.

9. Create a ritual that is meaningful to you to help you hear your calling or make it more tangible and visible to you. Consider the steps for ritual in this chapter, but redesign them as you see fit.

10. What gets you really excited or enthusiastic? List ten to twenty of those times in your life.

11. What are your gifts? In your journal, list at least twenty gifts.

12. What are your special skills and talents? In your journal, list at least fifty skills and talents.

13. Have you had a peak experience? Write about this time in detail to discover the elements that might indicate your calling. If you have had peak experiences more than once, what are their key features? Do you see a pattern?

14. When do you find yourself in *flow*? What tasks and challenges put you in this state? What patterns do you notice?

15. When are you most likely to participate, volunteer, or join in?

16. What groups or organizations do you belong to whose events you look forward to?

17. What charities or organizations do you donate to? If you could donate a lot more, what would be your first three choices?

18. What magazines do you subscribe to? If you looked at this list as if it belonged to someone else, what would it tell you?

19. What bumper stickers do you like?

20. When you pick up a newspaper, what do you look at first? What sections do you read? What do you ignore?

21. When you go into a bookstore, what section do you usually go to first?

22. What sites are you most likely to visit on the Internet?

23. What goes against your grain? What in your life feels as if it's *just not you*? What does this tell you?

# CHAPTER THIRTEEN

# First Steps and Strategies

Since it doesn't cost a dime to dream, you'll never short-change yourself when you stretch your imagination.

—Robert Schuller

I waited for the idea to consolidate, for the grouping and composition of themes to settle themselves in my brain. When I felt I held enough cards I determined to pass to action, and did so.

—Claude Monet

Accomplishing our purpose, becoming self-actualized, or fulfilling our destiny all sound like grand designs in need of grand plans. But all of us move through life in small increments and in small ways. What these small steps add up to can be the equivalent of climbing mountain ranges. Simple first steps can help us to achieve our bigger vision. Strategy is composed of many small components.

## A JOURNEY OF A THOUSAND MILES BEGINS WITH. . . .

. . . a single step.

How do you eat an elephant? One bite at a time.

How do you write a whole book? One word at a time, one page a day.

How do you make a big change? A little at a time, with tiny steps and great compassion for yourself. Get off track? Forget your way? Feel lost? Gently pull yourself back on the path without blame.

When we set our goals high or when we articulate our mission in words, we may feel small and helpless in the face of something so big and noble. What we want to do seems so far out of our reach, we don't even know if it's possible. We might fear we're immodest to even think of something so grand. We may have been told many times we were being unrealistic to believe we could do something of great value or make a difference in the world.

Chunking down our projects into manageable portions makes them possible to achieve.

Well begun is half done.

—Aristotle

## FIRST STEPS, BABY STEPS

When you have a clear idea of who you are and what you want to do, taking the first step may be the most difficult. You are more likely to have your vision of the *ultimate* success. You might have an image of someone who has achieved what you want to achieve, but no idea of how to proceed or get there. You may have no idea of the first step. Where do you begin?

As with any blueprint, the finished product has many of the hints for its creation. If you want to begin working in a certain field, you might investigate what kind of education and training it takes. You might then ask where you could get such training. What are the prerequisites? The cost? How long does it take? How do you get started?

The first step is often the hardest one because of our own fears and inertia. But in fact, it's often the easiest in terms of actual effort and time.

*The first step may be only a phone call.*

Where do you want to end up? Ask someone who has arrived there. If you have some idea of the kind of training you would need, start calling schools. Every time someone says, "I don't know," ask to be connected with someone who might know, or ask for the name and number of someone who knows. Start asking questions.

> The great breakthroughs in our lives generally happen
> only as a result of the accumulation of innumerable small
> steps and minor achievements.
>
> —Gregg Levoy

## ASK QUESTIONS

If your path isn't as directed as seeking schooling, seek answers from the school of experience. Talk to people who have done what you want to do. If you don't know anyone who has achieved your goal, try the local library or the Internet for ideas on where to go for information or materials to read. If you don't know what to ask, explain that you don't know what to ask. Ask people to tell you about whatever experience or goal they've achieved. Again, asking an open-ended question (remember about programming your dreams?) will often give you information you would never have learned with more direct and specific questions. You can later move to questions that are more specific.

"I see you donate doohickeys to needy children. How did that come about?"

"You went to a monastery in Tibet for three months? Please tell me how you got away!"

"You did that? Weren't you scared?"

"How do you manage to travel so much?"

"How did you get such a fantastic promotion?"

"You got a grant? How did you do that?"

Ask as many questions as you can think of. One answer will open another three questions.

Tell the person what you aspire toward, even if your idea is still nebulous or imprecise. Verbalizing your questions will help you formulate your ideas more clearly. The responses you receive may help shape your specific goals.

In every conversation, make sure to ask what your first step should be. It might start with something as simple as filling out an application from a specific agency. Ask people about their failures and mistakes, too. Ask about false starts, blind alleys, and possible obstacles. Remember, you're talking to someone who probably knows more than you do. Most important, you are talking with someone who has been down a similar path to the one you want to travel.

When you ask questions, you may sometimes not like the answers. When people ask me how to start writing and get published, I tell them to write every day. I suggest they start with a daily journal to find their voice and to begin to discover what they have to say. I suggest they take classes and workshops, and join or start a read-and-critique group. Frequently, they don't like these answers. They want to be writers, but they don't want to write! Or they don't want to show their writing to anyone. They just want it published.

When you've asked every question that you can think of, ask what they think you *should* have asked. Then ask them to answer that.

> The strategic adversary is fascism . . . the fascism in us all, in our heads and in our everyday behavior, the fascism that causes us to love power, to desire the very thing that dominates and exploits us.
>
> —Michel Foucault

## MENTORS, ROLE MODELS, AND COACHES

When you begin on a path, it is always better to have someone to talk to who has already traveled that route.

The people that you ask questions of may or may not become your mentors and coaches. But they are good to consider as possible mentors or role models.

A mentor is someone who has traveled the road you are about to embark on. This may be someone who teaches in the field or someone who has achieved the kind of success you long for. It may be a spiritual guide, a professor, an entrepreneur in an innovative business. A mentor will be willing to support you through your doubts, frustrations, and overcoming obstacles. He or she will be able to tell you what pitfalls to avoid and will see choices and opportunities that might escape your notice. He or she will be able to tell you how to be wary of certain dangers you might encounter, such as unscrupulous people offering services you don't need, calling themselves agents when they have no contacts, or misrepresenting themselves in some other way. A mentor can tell you what startup costs might be, what kind of licensure and insurance you'll need. He or she will know how long the lag phase is before you see a return from your efforts. He or she may tell you this project had better be a labor of love. A mentor will listen to you talk about the passion you share when everyone else doesn't want to hear another word about it.

A coach is a particular type of mentor who is more intimately involved in your project. He or she may give instruction that is more specific and take you through the steps one by one, rather than just supporting your own style of struggling. Some people use these terms interchangeably, but I think of a coach as someone who will help push me to my limits, who will encourage me to stretch myself when I'm frightened, and who will cheer me on. A coach takes a more active role.

Unlike a mentor or a coach whom you might speak to regularly, a role model can be someone you never meet. It might be a person who has currently reached a certain level of achievement, who overcame obstacles similar to your own, or someone whose biography inspired you to your own special form of greatness. It may be someone living or dead, famous or not. A role model embodies the traits and attributes that you aspire toward; he or she offers an image that you can emulate. Some people find it useful to think of their role model when they are having a rough time and ask themselves, "What would Madame Curie have done in this situation?" Although they can't really know what the role model would have done, entering this mind frame can offer a higher level of thought and coping skills.

In his books and tapes, Stephen Covey talks about people who have scripted us toward our best achievements. They believed in us when others didn't, and nurtured us along the way.

In his book *Callings*, author Gregg Levoy says:

People who understand the struggle involved in following a call may provide encouraging counsel that helps overcome the drag of inertia and fear because they've struggled with their own callings. You don't want advice from a "Do what I say, not what I do" type, but from those who are busy with calls of their own. They understand that when we talk about a calling, we're speaking of an encounter with divinity, with the deep soul, that must be honored. These people are most capable of propelling us into the greatest strides in growth and the profoundest changes in the course of our lives because they've witnessed and esteemed what is deepest in us. Even if we've cried wolf a time or two before, they also love us robustly, bear no major grudges against us, and take us seriously.

## ENLISTING A MENTOR OR COACH

While you don't have to ask someone to be a role model, it's best to approach someone you want to mentor you or to coach you and ask for the help you want.

Traditionally, people had mentors as part of their development. A person entering a trade signed on as an apprentice to a skilled crafts-person to learn the details of the profession. In modern times, with more formal education and people being so mobile, mentorships must be established more intentionally.

If you know of someone who has followed the path that you are about to embark on, ask whether he or she would be willing to mentor you. Since you are unlikely to know exactly what kind of help you will be needing at the start, you might ask this person what kind of help he or she can offer. Be aware that you are asking for a commitment of time and personal interest. The first person you ask may not be willing or able to offer, so understand that if the person declines, you don't have to take it personally. It doesn't mean he or she doesn't think this should be your purpose. It may only mean that this person doesn't think he or she is suited to be your mentor. When you ask your questions, be alert to the kind of person who can mentor you and who may be eager to do so. You may think you're imposing or bothering the person you approach, but people are often very happy to share their knowledge and be appreciated as an expert.

## 10 Steps for Finding a Mentor

1. Be alert to possible mentoring candidates.

2. Ask your friends who has mentored them or given them help.

3. Make a list of people you know who might mentor you.

4. Approach each person tentatively at first to test his or her receptivity.

5. If the person is agreeable, make your desires clear—what kind of mentoring do you want? How much time? How often? What knowledge? Ask what he or she might like to offer.

6. Be willing to hear no.

7. If you get a no, ask the person for suggestions of other people who might mentor you.

8. Consider having more than one mentor or coach for different aspects of your goals.

9. Be ready to move on to new mentors. As you progress and change, your needs will change.

10. Return this gift when someone approaches you when you're an expert. (It will be sooner than you think!)

## 16 Attributes of a Good Mentor

1. Supports your goals and choices without trying to impose his or her own

2. Provides a container for your vision and a possibly greater vision

3. Champions your independent thinking

4. Offers knowledge and information openly and without restriction

5. Gives corrective guidance and criticism in small doses that you can assimilate and put to use without being discouraged

6. Praises your talents and progress regularly

7. Demonstrates empathy and emotional support

8. Encourages you to have other mentors, role models, and guides

9. Does not try to make you a carbon copy of him or her

10. Allows you to work in an apprentice or protégé role without exploiting your time, talent, and labor for his or her own purposes

11. Does not charge fees for mentoring (unless this is part of the original agreement)

12. Models ethical and responsible behavior, including honesty and candor

13. Asks good questions to provoke new thought and ideas without imposing his or her own

14. Acknowledges your success without jealousy

15. Recognizes when you advance beyond him or her; is willing to learn from you

16. Allows you to go when you are ready

Trust and authenticity are part of a good mentoring relationship. Laurent A. Daloz, author of *Effective Teaching and Mentoring*, speaks eloquently to teaching and mentoring:

To engender trust is central to any strong, nurturant relationship. But while the trust that characterizes an early relationship owes much of its strength to the ascribed authority of the teacher, a more mature trust is sustained increasingly by the shared commitment of each partner. It must be constantly re-created. Like any living thing, trust wants tending. To keep it alive requires a small, but steady stream of risk—the will to drop the screen that protects our eyes from the full glare of another's presence. This is especially true as a relationship matures and the growing student asks more of the teacher's humanity. In the strength of a maturing trust, the partners are freer to challenge each other's ideas, knowing they are held by the mutual commitment. Conversely, with a diminishing need to protect a mask, each can afford to hear the other more fully and can learn more deeply. Thus the relationship becomes the caring context for the dialectic, the culture out of which a transforming synthesis can spring.

## Responsibilities of a Good Protégé

1. Respects the knowledge and experience of the mentor

2. Shows gratitude and appreciation

3. Respects the mentor's boundaries and need for privacy

4. Is considerate of the mentor's time and resources

5. Doesn't create crises to get extra attention

6. Is honest and forthcoming with the mentor

7. Asks questions and gives the mentor feedback, so the mentor has a clear idea of the protégé's needs

8. Remembers that mentors are only human beings and they have their own lives

Walter Truett Anderson, in *Reality Isn't What It Used to Be,* advises from another point of view, warning us what can happen when the mentor forgets his or her human imperfections:

Let us say—in a spirit of generosity to the countless people who have entered into such relationships over the millennia and will probably continue to do so—that this way of going after some of the more difficult kinds of wisdom is effective in some conditions and produces exactly the kind of results it should. Whether it does or doesn't, it is clearly a dangerous game.

The dangers are many. The teacher may exploit the student sexually, psychologically, or economically. The student may be taught a lot of seriously flawed wisdom if the teacher doesn't know as much as he thinks he does. Or the school may become a vehicle for the ego promotion of the teacher and his teachings. The teacher may metamorphose from a friend/mentor into guru-going-on-messiah. His writings may become scriptures, his sayings pearls of wisdom to be recorded and distributed to the world. The approach to teaching may become reified, turn into a thing with an institutionalized existence of its own.

Such warnings are well to keep in mind when choosing a mentor, teacher, or coach. While striving to be fully authentic and autonomous, we may abdicate our power to someone who awes us. This can happen with therapists, group leaders, and political figures—anyone in a position of power and authority to whom we look for leadership and guidance.

## TAKING ADVICE (OR NOT TAKING IT)

When you ask for help from others, they will probably give you advice—advice that has nothing to do with what you want to know, advice you didn't ask for, or advice that doesn't apply to you.

Certainly, enlisting a mentor or coach means you'll be getting lots of advice, and that's probably what you want. But remember that accepting advice is something that calls for discernment. Ask yourself whether this advice is helpful to you or actually applies to you. Ask yourself what consequences will come from following the advice. Whom does it serve? Does it *feel* right to you? Does this advice violate your boundaries or the professional ethics of your mentor's field? Is this direction in keeping with your goals and mission?

Discerning what advice—if any—is appropriate for you is a matter for your own judgment. Mentors who impose themselves on you against your wishes are no longer being helpful.

Always know that you don't have to take advice—no matter what the source.

## MOTIVATION

> With your spirit open and unconstricted, look at things
> from a high point of view.
> —Miyamoto Musashi (1584–1645),
> Samurai warrior

Taking your first steps on the path to realizing your purpose requires motivation. We tend to think that if we've found our true purpose, we'll automatically be motivated. But we like the comfort of the familiar, even when it's boring and unsatisfying. It's what we know! However, it doesn't challenge us. Change is always scary—even when it's a positive change, such as graduating from school, moving to a better home, or taking a long-awaited trip.

You can find the motivation to take those first difficult steps by looking at how you have been able to take the first steps for other things in your life. How did you get yourself to do it before? What worked for you to help you overcome your own tendency toward procrastination and inertia?

We all have to do things we don't like to do. For me, it's going to the dentist, having the oil changed in the car, getting a haircut, and doing my taxes. For some people, it might be doing laundry, mowing the lawn, or going to the office holiday party. But we do these tasks in spite of having a resistance to them—whatever the source of the resistance. How do we do it?

Knowing how you get yourself past your inclination to procrastinate can help you to take the first steps toward realizing your purpose. What do you tell yourself? What makes you get down to business and get the task done? Do you wait for the last minute? Does someone else have an influence? What is your personal style of motivating yourself?

People generally have three methods:

1. Focus on the negative consequences of not doing the task

2. Focus on the positive rewards of getting it done (including giving yourself a reward)

3. Employ some combination of the two, with the imagined outcome in pictures, sounds (words), or emotional and body states (feelings).

For example, I do my taxes—usually early—because I can't stand the thought of having that task hanging over my head. I also know that I *have* to do them or I'll get in trouble. I get the oil changed because I like to keep a car as long as possible and that's an important part of taking care of the car. I also don't want to get stuck somewhere because I didn't do basic maintenance.

These strategies fall into the first category. I'm avoiding the negative consequences, worries, and rotten feelings that come from postponing or not doing the tasks. However, I notice that I get myself to do other things that are sometimes more difficult by focusing on the positive rewards they will bring. I write because I know I will feel so good about myself for finishing my book. I want the pleasure of seeing my work published. By getting my books done, I know I will feel as if I've accomplished something with my life, that I did something of value, that I left something on the planet. That's strategy number two, focusing on the positive outcome and rewards of getting it done. For me, wanting to have published books is partly to avoid the negative consequence of being eighty or ninety years old and *hating* myself for not doing what I could have done. I imagine what it will be like to know my life is nearly over and that I wasted much of my time. That's not a feeling I want to experience! That's more of strategy number one—avoidance. Each day that I have trouble getting started with my writing, I think about how good I'll feel when I've finished my daily word quota—strategy number two.

So I use a combination of one and two—strategy number three—

with the emphasis changing depending on what I need to be motivated to do. My focus is also on a combination of the emotions I anticipate I will experience and on the visual pictures of the task being done, such as seeing my books stacked up in a big display in bookstores.

To find out what gets you motivated, review the many tasks you do every day that you would rather not do. Some people spend *most* of their day doing things they don't really want to do: completing tasks on the job they don't like (grunt work), doing chores at home, returning calls, paying bills, shopping for groceries, driving in traffic, and waiting in lines at gas stations, cleaners, pharmacies, and banks. How do you get yourself to do these things? What do you tell yourself to get yourself to do it? Do you need a deadline? Do you worry about someone else being angry with you if you don't do it? Do you do things only to keep yourself from being fired from your job? Do you do things to feel proud of yourself, to bask in the joy of a job well done? Do you do them to just get them out of the way so you can move on to something else you really like? Do you give yourself rewards for getting things done?

How do you do this? Do you make pictures in your mind of the outcome (positive or negative)? Do you anticipate hearing the voices of people harping at you if you don't get something done? Do you focus on the feelings, emotions, or body reactions (a warm rush, stomach clenching, anxiety, headaches) that you'll experience by doing or not doing the particular task? The more you know the detailed style of your thinking and self-talk, the more you can use what works to motivate yourself when you want to.

Being aware of your particular style of self-talk will help you discover the many strategies you have *already* developed that help you move beyond your desire to do nothing at all! You already have skills to deal with your inertia, fears, and laziness. Human beings are studies in contrasts—we are caught in the opposing forces of wanting to move toward our highest potential on the one hand and degenerating into sloppiness on the other. The methods that already keep you functioning and productive are the clues to your own personal style of motivation.

## COURAGE OR CAUTION

Making a big change takes courage. We naturally fear change because we are evolutionarily predisposed to want to stay safe and comfortable. It has survival value. No need to cross the river and look for food and game if there is plenty right here. Why take the risk?

But humans also want to venture out, to stretch and make discoveries, to move beyond our borders both inside and outside:

"I wonder what's on the other side of the ocean."

"What could be on the other side of the moon?"

"What would happen if I mixed this stuff with that liquid?"

And so we make progress as a species. (Or we don't make progress, depending on how you evaluate the discovery and its use.)

On a personal level, we also have the desire to be all we can be and stretch beyond the limits others have set for us or we have set for ourselves, staying in our comfort zone.

"What could my life be like if I did that?"

"What new experiences could I have if I went there?"

"What might I learn about myself if I try this?"

"What interesting person might I meet if I went to that event alone?"

It takes courage to do something different and move beyond the familiar. Courage comes from what motivates you: the satisfaction of an accomplishment, the high praise and monetary rewards of certain kinds of achievement, a better life.

Real courage comes with some caution. Too much caution will keep you stuck and will prevent you from doing anything new. How cautious do you need to be? How courageous can you be before you start doing stupid or dangerous things?

To be able to venture courageously but sensibly into new territory—in the world or in our own minds—means being able to calculate the risks of what we do: a mixture of courage and caution in the right proportions.

> For most tribal people, the risk was not so much one of dying but of not living properly. It was the quality of your time on Earth, not the quantity, that was important. How different that dream from the one I had been taught!
>
> —John Perkins

## CALCULATING RISK AND CONSEQUENCES

Every time we step outside our doors, we risk having all kinds of terrible things happen to us. Even staying home has its risks; so many accidents can happen in your own home. Fearing the worst, we can hide inside, play it safe, and not venture into new territory.

All life is risk. If you're not taking risks, you're really not living; you're as good as dead. Each time we do venture out, we are deciding that where we are going is important enough to risk the various possible consequences. We do this mostly unconsciously, and some of us do it more than others. The way we take precautions in our exposure (financially, emotionally, sexually), the way we drive, the time of day or night, the places we go to, are all examples of calculated risk.

In venturing into something new and scary, the risk factors loom larger than they might for a trip to the supermarket. We don't know what to expect, and the unknown is always more scary than the known.

Again, a mentor who has taken this journey and who can anticipate some of the obstacles and pitfalls you are likely to encounter will be helpful. Mentors will encourage you to move beyond your fears—especially when they may be irrational. They can help you calculate the risks that can be identified and support you through those times when you just can't know how it will turn out. A mentor can show you how to live with ambiguity.

> If it's a good idea . . . go ahead and do it. It is much easier
> to apologize than it is to get permission.
>
> —Grace Murray Hopper

## IF YOU THINK IT'S TOO LATE—AND OTHER EXCUSES

Perhaps your desires still scare you. You've found yourself thinking of all the reasons why you're not going to be able to take your first steps. These are typical reasons given for not taking the first steps to realize your dreams:

## The Usual Excuses

I don't have the:

| | |
|---|---|
| Money | Personality |
| Time | Confidence |
| Experience | Training/knowledge |
| Support | Space |
| Self-discipline | Energy |
| Courage | |

Or:

I'm too: old, fat, stupid, clumsy, poor, or young.
I'm not talented.
I might fail.
Others would discourage (laugh at, criticize) me.
I would feel foolish, awkward, and self-conscious.
I'll do it when things aren't so busy, hectic, and crazy.
I'll do it when I lose weight.
I'll do it when I feel better and I'm not so depressed.
My kids (job, spouse, parents) come first.
I've never done anything like it.
It's too weird.
My family (friends, colleagues, spouse, children) will disapprove.
I don't have the right credentials.
I don't have the right connections.
It's already been done.
The odds are against me.
It's too hard.
How could I ever be that terrific?
I might do it and *still* be unhappy.
I'm afraid.

You can add your own excuses and obstacles to this list. Notice how all of this self-talk discourages you from taking action, keeps you down, *and keeps you feeling lousy!*

I thought about the many times I had worried about a future event, only to discover that it was not nearly as threatening as I had expected. I realized that the fear is often nothing more than the anticipation of pain. It is a dream—a nightmare—that is probably based on some association with a memory or another event in the past— another dream—that somehow appears to be connected with the one we expect in the future. Indeed, by changing the dream, either the one in the past or the one in the future, we can alleviate—or amplify—the fear.

—John Perkins

## PERCEIVED OBSTACLES: INTERNAL OR EXTERNAL?

Again, we may see our obstacles as external—coming from outside us in the form of other people's opinions and needs or circumstances that feel beyond our control (our age or class). Alternatively, we may see the blocks as internal—created by our beliefs about ourselves or our beliefs about the way the universe works. In fact, most obstacles are created internally because whatever is external (what others do or say) must pass through our interpretive process, which is often just plain wrong—for example, "I can't go back to school because so-and-so will be upset with me." We can never know that unless we check out our assumptions, but most of us never do. We assume that our assumptions and interpretations are reality—out there—instead of a story we made up.

What are the obstacles that you see in your way of your dream and how might you see them differently? For example, "I'm too old" can be rephrased as, "I have life experience and the wisdom that comes with that. Doing this now offers me judgment, persistence, and patience I didn't have when I was younger."

## THIN THINGS

Stephen Covey says that all we get caught up "in the thick of thin things." When I first heard this statement in the context of his *The 7 Habits of Highly Effective People* audiotapes, I thought of the many empty, time-wasting things I did (and often still do) that ate up my precious hours. I was living as if I would live forever, instead of being mindful of the reality that I have a finite number of hours to do whatever it is I am here to do. Making small talk on the telephone, going out with people whose company is unhealthy for me, watching television shows that add nothing to my education or level of consciousness, and a myriad of other behaviors were eating up my life. The days were going by faster and faster the older I got (everyone seems to notice this at some point), and I wasn't doing what I had always assumed I would do. I looked around to see others who were still talking about what they would do someday (travel, write, paint, volunteer for the causes they believed in) and who weren't doing it. It was clear to me that most of them were *never* going to do these things because they weren't even taking the first steps. *And I was never going to get to my mission either if I let all the thin things in my life eat up my limited time.*

This simple idea was a life-changing event for me. It was one of those revelations that seem so ordinary. "Yes, of course it's so," we say about so many simple and wise ideas, but then we continue as we were before. This time, it was an inner knowing that vibrated inside me, that echoed through my days and woke me out of my sleep at night. I asked myself what, exactly, my thin things were. Then I set about limiting them, delegating them, or eliminating them altogether. I saw how much busy work I'd filled my life with and I made some immediate changes.

I'm still working on eliminating busy work. Now I know why some artists' homes are so messy. They have more important things to do than "thin things" like dashing to straighten up the house every five minutes.

What are the thin things that keep you from doing what you most want to do? What can you change, quit, or do less often? Who else might take on chores that are important to them but not to you?

By eliminating clutter from your day, you will make time, space, energy, and even money for your special, unique dream of your future.

## CRITICISM AND MIRRORS

As we introduce changes in our lives, we can expect other people to object to them. As Harriet Lerner says, they will want us to "Change back!" They will say, "You've really changed!" and they won't mean it as a compliment. They will be angry that we are no longer so available to do what they want, to support them in their thin things so that they won't hear their own callings.

It is a cliché in today's self-help movement that criticism is really a mirror. What others find as faults in us are often their own. They will call us selfish when we take time to be alone and to be creative, but what they are really saying is they would feel selfish if they did that. They don't like seeing our independence or authenticity because they will have to see how much they've ignored their personal dreams.

The mirror works both ways. What drives me most crazy about someone is likely to be how much his or her behavior reminds me of what I don't like in myself.

When you are tempted to be critical and judgmental of others, when they drive you crazy by their behavior, remember that this tells you something about yourself. Those hot buttons offer information about your own struggle.

We find fault with or shun people whom we've "outgrown." We recoil from our earlier levels of foolishness and immaturity. We are embarrassed by our old blunders, mistakes, and lack of wisdom and understanding. We don't want to be reminded of where we were—and, oh, not so very long ago. Robert Kegan, in *The Evolving Self,* says there is nothing so unattractive to us as the stage of development we just left.

Criticism—given or received—is often in the category of, "You'd better stop drinking. Your face is getting all blurry."

## BALANCE

In taking our first steps, we are taking action toward answering our call. Such action, scary as it is by definition, needs to be balanced with other activities, giving us time to assimilate what we've learned and the changes we experience. If we could simply put one foot in front of the other until we were only running in a forward direction, we would have done it long before now. We wouldn't need mentors, coaches, guidance, and self-help books.

So we need to balance our drive toward our goals and missions with time to pull back, to reflect, rethink, reevaluate, and just *be*. Balance means doing things unrelated to the main thrust of our lives. Even the lion sleeps twenty hours a day. We also need to withdraw and listen to our inner voices between arduous expeditions into the unknown.

Balance should be tailored to your individual needs and style. It may take the form of quiet and solitude, such as meditation; as play time; or as something physical and active if your mission is more mental or emotional.

For me, yoga classes balance my mental pursuits of reading, writing, and poetry. I find that a very strenuous style of hatha yoga gets me out of my head and into my body. It relieves the stiffness I get from sitting still reading or typing at the computer. If my project were building or carpentry, I might choose listening to and playing music or going to movies as balance.

## FLEXIBILITY

Part of balance is flexibility. We move forward with the understanding that we can change our minds, that as more facts are revealed, we may have to change our plans or our methods. We may end up doing something that was different from our original vision because we have learned what works, what is needed, or something more satisfying along the way.

This is not the same as being distracted from our goals or losing our way on the journey. Conscious flexibility allows us to take advantage of new opportunities, teachers, and ideas as they come along. When we are open and flexible, we are willing to use new knowledge, skills, and ideas to move in new directions—directions we could never have anticipated when we set out.

## ALTERNATE PLANS, PARACHUTES, AND CONTINGENCY STRATEGIES

While we cannot predict the course of our journeys or what dragons await us along the way, we *can* have some plans to deal with emergencies and problems that we can anticipate. Our mentors and role models can be particularly helpful here. They can tell us what problems they had and were unprepared for. We are unlikely to have the same problems, but a knowledge of the most common difficulties can be helpful. We can have alternate strategies to deal with categories of specific problems. We can have parachutes ready in case we have to jump.

Depending on your venture, this may be some variation on "Don't quit your day job." It may mean having enough financial resources to see you through five years of no income in a brand-new business that people don't even understand. (Look at the ridicule of the idea of a personal computer when they first came out.) It may mean you will need an inordinate amount of patience until you get any recognition. (Stephen King wrote for twelve years before his first book was published.) Your mission may contradict the belief system and power of established authorities and require enormous persistence and fortitude. (Consider the derision Charles Darwin and Galileo faced.)

## THE LEARNING CURVE

When beginning a new way of life or returning to an old one we lost, we may expect to step forward and have everything go smoothly. People start their art or music lessons and expect a level of proficiency that usually takes years to accomplish. I regularly hear from people who want to write a book and expect to get it published *and* to make a lot of money. A beginner often doesn't know that most authors write several books before one is published. Beginners don't realize how much skill and practice and expertise it takes. To the neophyte, craft seems effortless.

When we take our first steps into a new domain and a new way of living, we can never foresee the many holes in our knowledge and understanding. We may not expect that to sell our product or service we will also have to learn about bookkeeping, marketing, public relations, advertising, and all the other aspects of running a business. If we begin a spiritual practice, we may not count on the usual struggles along the path: doubts, uncertainties, fear, loss of focus, and confusion.

Difficulties are part of the learning curve. Remember when you first learned how to read? To ride a bike? To drive a car? Remember how hard and complicated it seemed? Hopefully, we are learning throughout our lives, and will overcome initial difficulties.

## REDEFINING FAILURE

There is something so negative about the word *failure* that I have resisted using it here. But while some people think of failure as disastrous and shameful, as ruination and humiliation, I want to say that *if you're not failing on a regular basis, you're not taking enough risks. And if you're not taking risks, you're not living!*

Most successful businesspeople have had several businesses fail before they were successful—and often some had failed businesses *while* they were successful. Mistakes are how we learn. When we learn what doesn't work, we can do more of what does work. We can experiment to see what works best, knowing that many of our tries will fail.

Mistakes, errors, blunders, and failures are all part of the learning curve. People who succeed in realizing their dreams and becoming all they know they can be are those who persist through the rough spots. They know that failures are part of their education. And without failures and struggles of all kinds, success wouldn't be as sweet.

There is only one success: to be able to live your life in
your own way.

—Christopher Morley

## DREAMS INTO ACTION

1. What are the first questions you need to ask to begin your journey?

2. Where can you seek the answers?

3. What are the smallest first steps you can take?

4. Make a list of your first ten steps and write the first three on
   your calendar as appointments with yourself.

5. Whom do you most admire? Why? Make a list of these people and their best attributes.

6. Make a list of the people you know who might mentor you.
   Write down the questions you'd like to ask them.

7. List five tasks or chores that you have to do regularly, but
   don't like to do.

8. How do you get yourself to do these things that you don't
   like or that are hard for you? Make some notes of the strategies that work for you (making pictures, sounds, or focusing
   on feelings; avoiding the negative consequences of not doing
   the task or looking forward to the positive outcomes of getting it done). You are likely to use a variety of strategies that
   change depending on the circumstances. Notice what works
   best.

9. How can you transfer these strategies that already work for
   you into realizing your dream or purpose?

10. What risks are involved in the first steps of your journey?

11. Examine whatever obstacles you perceive: internal or external, real or imagined. What are your best strategies for dealing with them?

12. How do these obstacles—or your perception of them as obstacles—serve you? (Remember, all behavior is purposeful.)

13. What self-talk is keeping you from taking first steps or stopping you along the way? Rescript these messages to yourself. Make this a journal entry.

14. As Stephen Covey says, we all get caught up "in the thick of thin things." What are the *thin things* you are doing instead of what is most important to you? Make a list of at least ten. Mark those you can delegate to others (D), eliminate (E), or reduce (R) in frequency.

15. Who are your critics?

16. What boundaries do you need to set to put a stop to their discouraging words? What do you need to say to them? (You can silence the critics that come in your self-talk, too.)

17. Can you convert your critics into helpers by changing the way you interpret what they say?

18. What is out of balance in your life?

19. What do you need to do to make a change toward more balance?

20. Whom do you know that you consider to have a balanced life? What can you emulate?

21. What would help you cultivate flexibility?

22. Choose a role model whose flexibility you respect. What does this person do and say? When you are feeling stuck or rigid,

ask yourself what this person would do in your situation and do that, even if it feels weird.

23. What are your alternate strategies and plans for your journey?

24. What kinds of learning curves have you already experienced?

25. List steps that you expect to be part of your learning curve.

26. Can you laugh at your own blunders and errors? How do you have to change your thinking so that you can?

27. What "failures" in your life have been the most educational?

# CHAPTER FOURTEEN

# Writing a Mission Statement

A man to carry on a successful business must have imagination. He must see things as in a vision, a dream of the whole thing.

—Charles Schwab

I didn't have anybody, really, no foundation in life, so I had to make my own way. Always, from the start. I had to go out in the world and become strong, to discover my mission in life.

—Tina Turner

A mission statement provides the blueprint for the kind of future we want to have, starting with the present. Writing a mission statement provides vision and tenacity. It takes us through the hazards and anxieties of moving into our most satisfying future. Through our busy days, innumerable distractions, and responsibilities, it is a reminder to stay focused on our own lives.

Writing a mission statement requires us to think clearly about what is important. We may feel we know what is important, what our values, goals, and purpose are, but until we put it into words, we can't hear these as one coherent whole. Writing a mission statement means we have to order our thoughts, make sense of them, and make them clear to ourselves, as well as anyone else with whom we might share them.

Also, the act of writing makes the mission concrete. It makes it real. Like a mission statement in business, a written personal mission statement is a commitment of purpose. By writing it down, we have made a contract with ourselves.

In a way, writing a mission statement is an act of ritual. It speaks powerfully to our unconscious that we take ourselves seriously, that we mean what we say. It is an invocation of our deepest dreams and our sense of ourselves as unique and valuable. A written mission statement takes our mission from inside to outside, making it visible not just to others, but to ourselves.

## MISSION STATEMENT AS SELF-TALK

A mission statement is self-talk at its highest level. We say to ourselves what is important. We say what we are, what we are *for,* and what our lives are about. A mission statement contains our highest values and our deepest desires for the expression of our unique gifts. It expresses our passion for life and the way we want to live it. It is imbued with enthusiasm, gusto, and confidence. It says, "I *can* do this. I *will* do this!"

Gregg Levoy, in his book *Callings,* addresses this issue eloquently:

You don't want an answer you can put in a box and set on a shelf. You want a question that will become a chariot to carry you across the breadth of your life, a question that will offer you a lifetime of pondering, that will lead you toward what you need to know for your integrity, draw to you what you need for your journey, and help you understand what it means to burst at the seams.

Self-talk is a regular part of our daily lives. Writing a mission statement is a way to take that natural inclination to talk to ourselves and do it in a way that brings out our best, reinforces our goals, and keeps us on our chosen path. It turns our self-talk into the voice of our higher selves. It champions us and cheers us on.

## DISTINGUISHING GOALS FROM MISSION

Many people confuse goals with a mission. Achieving your goals is part of the process of living your mission. With new information and experiences, goals may be completed, changed, or discarded. A mission statement transcends day-to-day goals and tasks.

A mission statement contains more than the narrow desires of your self, but reaches into your Self—that part of you that includes spirit and cosmos, that is part of the divine—whatever that means to you. Once again, as with any personal ritual, there is no need to have a religious belief system. You can be a skeptic, an agnostic, or an atheist, and still have a sense of a transcendent part of the Self that you want to express in the short time you have to live.

If you think of your mission as the apex of a pyramid, you will see that goals, along with values, tasks, and strategies, are among the steps toward your goal. (See the figure on page 245.) You might prefer to think of these elements as concentric circles, with your mission at the center—the core of all you do.

## ELEMENTS OF AN EXCEPTIONAL MISSION STATEMENT

A good mission statement addresses all the major areas of your life. These have been described in various ways to include body, mind, and spirit; to address social, creative, emotional, and intellectual needs; and to satisfy the categories of love and work.

I suggest five categories, which you might want to emphasize to different degrees. You may want to expand or narrow these as it suits you to express your personal mission statement.

1. Physical (your body, including health, exercise, diet, rest)

2. Interpersonal (your social contacts, including friends, family, colleagues, lovers)

3. Intrapersonal (your relationship with yourself, what you say to yourself, how you manage your emotions and behavior, your need for solitude)

4. Intellectual (your mental challenges and educational goals, your thoughts and beliefs, your expression of creativity in work and play)

5. Spiritual (your relationship to the transcendent, whether you express that in terms of a divinity, nature, or the cosmos)

In Stephen Covey's model, there are four categories: physical, social, mental, and spiritual. He groups items 3 and 4 together under *mental*. You might want to expand the intrapersonal to separate emotion (feelings) and thought (cognition). That distinction is important in some mission statements in order to encourage the development of a balance of these two elements of the intrapersonal mode.

There are other ways to group the life issues that may be part of our mission statements. Howard Gardner, in *Frames of Mind: The Theory of Multiple Intelligences,* suggests that we have eight intelligences (expanded from his previous seven): verbal, mathematical/logical, spatial, kinesthetic, musical, interpersonal, intrapersonal, and (the add-on) naturalistic—pertaining to a knowledge and awareness of things in nature.

A good mission statement contains the three elements of our existence: to be, to do, and to have. What do you want to be? What do you want to do? What do you want to have? In many ways, throughout this book, you have already asked yourself those questions.

Stephen Covey suggests we ask ourselves what legacy we want to leave. He says that a good mission statement unifies our various roles in life, connecting and integrating our subpersonalities.

Asking yourself what you want to have is not a question about material possessions. Many people make the mistake of thinking that owning more and better material things will bring them happiness, but nobody says they wish they had a bigger house when they learn they are close to death. By *having,* I am asking you to consider other values. Some people might, as part of their mission, seek to have greater peace of mind or peace in their families. Their mission might include something about having more kindness, tolerance, and compassion or having more resilience in the face of failure and disappointment. In this case, the *haves* are more psychological or spiritual. They are at a higher level of consciousness and enlightenment than the *haves* of acquisitiveness and material possessions.

A mission statement is for you personally, not to impress others or for anyone else's approval. For that reason, it should be in your own language. By that, I mean more than your native language. Use your everyday speech; express your personal passions in metaphors that call to you. It may be as short as a single sentence or as long as several pages. It may be in bulleted phrases or in paragraphs. Some mission statements might include diagrams or drawings, if that is how your vision is expressed.

You might think of the classic questions you were taught to address in writing any piece:

Who?     Where?
What?    When?
Why?     How?

A mission statement is action-oriented and gives you a clear idea of what you have to do and be to accomplish the mission. It has verbs that can be translated into goals and behaviors (educate, activate, create, build, direct), it has a target (you, others, your community, your planet), and it conveys your values. For example, your mission might be to build a retreat center. There you could teach meditation and dreamwork, or you could train terrorists. What are the values behind your vision? What does it offer others? What does it do or express to the world and all its inhabitants? How does it make the world better?

Paradoxically, a good mission statement is at once specific and ambiguous. You may know what your mission is and what you want to do, but there will be many ways to go about it. A good mission statement allows for this flexibility. There is room for evolution, change, and growth within it. Thinking that you've "got it" will close you off to making changes when they are needed and will blind you to new truths as they emerge.

Once written, a mission statement should be lived, something that is with you on a daily basis, a reminder of what your life is about and a reminder of who and what you really are and what you stand for. It is your personally tailored guide for making decisions about goals and plans. When you feel you are stumbling, uncertain of what to do, in doubt about your choices, your mission can be your beacon to keep you on your chosen path, to remind you what you decided was most important to you. It exemplifies the ethical code and standards you most want to live by.

## MENTORS, ROLE MODELS, AND
## SUPPORT SYSTEMS

Your mission can be encouraged by those people who are role models and supports in your life. Your mentor is only one of these people. Sharing your mission statement with those closest to you, especially family and those you love, can be part of making it real. Stephen Covey suggests that each member of a family write his or her own mission statement and then create a family mission statement that you carve out together—not one handed down by anyone who sees himself or herself as head of the household.

Enlisting family or friends is part of establishing support in your daily life. Those who know us and care for us can be recruited to keep us on track, to remind us of our dreams and our mission. We can ask them to confront us when we get off track, and we can urge their cooperation toward making the time and space so that not only can we realize our missions—they can realize theirs.

## REVIEW AND PERIODIC REVISION

A good mission statement is not something you can compose in an hour or two. Because it should contain all the aspects of your life, it might take hours and weeks to formulate your basic ideas and put them all together. Periodically, you will go back to your statement to revise it and add to it. As you change, with new experiences and new learning, so will your mission. Allow yourself room for change and growth. If you think of your mission statement as written in concrete, then you will have simply traded one set of traps for another. A mission statement lives in you and with you, breathing, changing, and growing as you do.

A mission statement:

1. Speaks to you of your passions and purpose

2. Contains your values and ethics

3. Is in your own language, metaphors, and speech pattern

4. Is personally tailored to your highest values

5. Encompasses all parts, roles, and subpersonalities in your life

6. Details what you are *for*, rather than what you are against

7. Contains action and direction that can be shaped into goals and plans

8. Is a beacon to keep you moving on your chosen path

9. Contains what you want to be, do, and have (material and nonmaterial)

10. Transcends the self—includes others and the planet

11. Encourages further change, growth, and development

# 8 Guidelines for Writing a Mission Statement

1. List your values.

2. Choose three to five most cherished values from your list.

3. How do you want to express these values in the world? Choose action verbs.

4. Toward whom is your mission directed? Who is your audience?

5. What outcome will your mission accomplish?

6. How is your mission a part of you? State this in terms of what you are *for*.

7. Make sure your mission includes the five basic areas of your life:

   a. Physical
   b. Interpersonal
   c. Intrapersonal
   d. Intellectual
   e. Spiritual

8. What would your obituary say if you had lived your mission?

## SAMPLE MISSION STATEMENTS

### Mission Statement
### Alexandra McGee
### Female, age 30, member of Twin Oaks
### Community,* three years of revising
### mission statement

*In order to help others, I need to be a healthy, centered person. I want to promote intentional community, live yoga, and teach yoga. I want to be around loved ones, in beautiful places. I want to nurture a positive local setting with world peace in mind.*

*In order to help others, I need to be a healthy, centered person.*
I will learn to know my center and act from it. I want to be an agent of calm and centeredness for others and help them find where and how they can live happily. I will spend quiet, reflective time each week to allow my values to resurface. Any time I feel deep emotions or insights, I will allow the "old woman" to have time to cradle me. I will not flee from pain or grief.

---

* Twin Oaks Community is an intentional egalitarian community of approximately eighty adults and fifteen children on 460 acres in central Virginia, established in 1967. For more information, go to *http://www.twinoaks.org/.*

*To promote intentional community*
I want all people to know about the alternative called intentional community. I will use my writing, social, and organizing skills to support the communal movement. I want many communities to learn lessons from each other, refer to each other, bolster each other in time of need: money and reputation crises.

*Live yoga, and teach yoga.*
I will have a discipline of yoga and spend 30 percent of my waking time outdoors. I will seek education on yoga through books, teachers, and videos. I want to help others learn simplicity and reliance on inner Source, not external gain.

*I want to be around loved ones, in beautiful places.*
I want to spend time playing with friends and maintaining our relationships. I want to be kind and compassionate in my deed and manner. I want to support and be supported by another person with whom I make a commitment.

*I want to nurture a positive local setting with world peace in mind.*
I will only try to act where my actions will make a long-term difference. I will be organized and live out my values efficiently. I strive for easy travel and a safe home. I will model simple, cooperative living. I want to preserve natural places.

## MISSION STATEMENT
### Carolina Small
### Female, age 28, mortgage processor

*I want my life to be EXTRAORDINARY.*
I always give thanks to God Almighty for the experiences I live every day and reconfirm my absolute faith in him as the Creator of this wonderful world.

I want to feel every day the inner motivation to live with enthusiasm and satisfaction.

I want to be beautiful and feel good about myself, inside and outside. I care about my health and outlook.

I want to search for excellence but avoid being a perfectionist.

I want to laugh more and keep afloat my good sense of humor.

I always recognize I am lucky and I am proud of being who I am. I value my way of thinking and deserve the best in life.

I want to be surrounded by genuine and valuable people that make me want to share my time with them and show them my love in a simple and healthy way.

I avoid and keep away negative and false people that come my way without thinking twice.

I want to keep my things organized and in good condition.

I avoid procrastination: I want, I can, I do it.

When I establish and work for my goals:

I have clearly in my mind what I want.

I think thoroughly what benefits I will get.

I identify the sources I can count on.

I consider the different options and I take advantage of my privilege and power of decision.

I accept my mistakes and learn from them.

I enjoy, learn and celebrate from my success.

I want to remember and reconfirm that I am #1 in my life. My needs are above everything and everybody.

I want to live my life to the fullest, today and now. I enjoy my blessings. I avoid thoughts of criticism about other people's life. As long as it does not affect me, their decisions are theirs and everyone is responsible for solving their problems. I will only help when I can. I am not responsible for anybody's happiness; I only can give the happiness that comes out from my soul and my heart. I will base my thoughts and will act in favor of other people's well-being as long as these actions are to my complete satisfaction and well-being.

I express what I want and think assertively. I hear advice but will not allow other people's beliefs to affect me.

I will keep searching for sources of inspiration and admiration that influence me positively and that connect me even more with my vision of the future.

Every day, I try to do the things I like, how I like (at least 3 of them):

- Talk to a loved one or a friend.
- Sing a song by heart.
- Have a conversation with a little kid.
- Massage my body.
- Exercise my mind with meditation.
- Ride my bike.
- Go to the park.
- Listen to music (listen to the words).
- Eat something delicious.
- Go to the library.
- Watch a complete program on TV.
- Play tennis.
- Go to the movies or rent videos.
- Play a game.
- Dance.
- Surf the Internet.
- Do something completely new to me.
- Do anything that makes me feel good in the moment.

Notice the ordinary heartfelt language of the following mission statement, which he sent me by E-mail.

## MISSION STATEMENT
## Jake Kawatski
## Male, age 48, member of Twin Oaks Community

As for a personal mission statement: I suppose I most cherish the "golden rule" (Do unto others, as you would have them do to you).

Coming from a big family, I have always enjoyed working with kids, but decided years ago that I didn't need to bring any more children into the world. I made a promise to be a doting uncle, and have also enjoyed teaching part-time for about twenty years (as well as being a meta [child care worker] for 6 years at Twin Oaks). It has been a source of pleasure to see them mature into sensible adults (for the most part) particularly in the case of "problem kids" whom we fretted over in many a meta meeting. I firmly believe, "It takes a whole village to raise a child" and had chosen Twin Oaks, in large part, because it has nearly always had a wide spectrum of ages, and I could be around kids, without being a dad.

My joy in being with young people carries over to my perennial wonder at the reemergence of new life in spring. I never fail to be amazed at the miracle in the seed, having nurtured gardens in many different climates, since I was a toddler. Some of my dearest friends and relatives also share this green passion. I'm 48 now, and don't have the physical stamina I had to garden like I did. I limit myself to mornings only. (Mad dogs and Englishmen go out in the noonday sun!) In the sultry Virginia summer afternoons, I've taken up indexing texts in the past five years: a welcome chance to read new books and relax in the shade and get paid for it!

I'd like to have people remember me for my sense of joy and silliness. As dedicated as I am to my work, I value my ability to stand back from it all on occasion and "cut loose." Someone said, "By the time you're 50, you have the face you deserve!" When I look in the mirror at my aging self, I don't see wrinkles, only laugh lines.

## MY OBITUARY

As I wrote the first draft of this chapter, I had an experience that few people encounter. I got a call from a woman in my writing class to tell me there was an obituary in the newspaper with my name. She thought I might be receiving a lot of phone calls, since the woman's age wasn't listed. She lived in Pompano Beach, a city very close to Fort Lauderdale, and it was possible that people could mistake her obituary for mine.

The content of the obituary was simple: Joan Mazza, Pompano Beach, died February 21, 1999. It said nothing of the woman, her age, cause of death, her family, or who she was. The next sentence gave the location and time of the wake and funeral.

You might say I looked at this and felt as if I had another chance at life. This woman died on the day before my fifty-first birthday. I looked at that empty obituary and knew I wanted mine to say a lot more. I would want it to list the books I'd written, the people whose lives I'd touched, how I had made a difference in the world. I wanted it to say that someone would miss me. I wanted it to say I was a teacher, poet, and artist, as well as a writer of self-help books. I wanted it to say—somehow—that I had left a legacy. As I gazed at the paper, I said out loud, "I'd better get busy."

None of us know how long we have. What do you want your obituary to say?

## DREAMS INTO ACTION

1. Using your journal entries and answers from the previous exercises, what do you see as your mission today?

2. What have you always wanted to do, but never said out loud—not even to yourself?

3. What have you always wanted to do, but never got around to—yet?

4. When you are ninety, what will you regret that you didn't do in your life?

5. What legacy do you want to leave?

6. What do you want people to say about you at your funeral?

7. Imagine your obituary in the newspaper. What do you want it to say? Write it now.

8. Imagine seeing your biography in print. What would it say so far? What do you want it to say?

9. What is the first thing you must do to write your mission statement?

10. What are you *for*?

11. What do you know how to do better than almost anyone you know?

12. Begin writing your mission statement now. Even a sentence or two can open the door to the life you want for yourself.

# CHAPTER FIFTEEN

# Conclusion: Dream Back Your Life

When you cease to dream you cease to live.
—Malcolm Forbes

Let me tell you the secret that has led me to my goal.
My strength lies solely in my tenacity.
—Louis Pasteur

Our dreams, whether sleeping or waking, provide information we can use. By reviewing the techniques offered in this book and using them on a regular basis, we can approach our highest goals and be in control of our own lives and our own destiny. We can be all that we know we were meant to be.

This book has been about listening to yourself—hearing what your body, emotions, and fleeting thoughts tell you about yourself. It has been an intentional journey into the power of your own mind—in several different stages of consciousness, including both waking and sleeping.

## TAKING CHARGE OF YOUR OWN LIFE

You know you have many choices, many ways to see the events of your life and the way you interpret them. You know that you can choose or not choose to do things that may open up your conscious mind to deeper layers and to the core of who you are.

In many ways, there is no core, only what you construct out of your beliefs and experiences, your wishes and fears. You can, many say, re-construct yourself or re-create yourself to be who you want to be.

By choosing to emphasize your talents and skills, your abilities and willingness to learn, you can develop a vision of a future that begins with every choice you make today.

Sometimes, the next stage of our development calls for us to let go of old ways, old beliefs, and old habits. Others close to us may find the changes we make alarming or inconvenient for them.

Some of your changes may seem sacrilegious—even to you. But Wal-ter Truett Anderson informs us in *The Future of the Self: Inventing the Postmodern Person* that there are Zen monasteries where the ancient Bud-dhist scriptures are used as toilet tissue. "Nothing is more highly valued in the esoteric traditions than walking away from dogmas."

Dreaming back your life may mean you need to walk away from some old dogmas. What are they?

## VISION

Much of what we do and how we do it in our lives depends upon our language and how we phrase it. A single word can draw one person in with enthusiasm and cause another to recoil. Perhaps the idea of having a vision for yourself is more appealing than a mission or a pur-pose. This is your life and you get to shape it as you see fit. After all, that's what this whole book has been about—finding your own way in your own style to be who you are. What is your vision of who you are? What is your vision of who you want to be?

As you develop your vision, know that we are always in flux, always growing, changing, and seeing the world and ourselves differently. Nei-ther we nor our mission statements can be securely fixed. We must always be willing to change and grow as our circumstances and our changing perceptions call for it.

Walter Truett Anderson, in *The Future of the Self*, says:

Society is not going to find an overarching moral code, spiritual or secular, that will work uniformly for everybody. Not all individuals are going to find clear moral identities. What we have to do, whether we do it singly or collectively, is find ways that people can learn how to be responsible in this kind of world.

Our identities evolve with the times, the people with whom we choose to interact, and all of our moment-to-moment choices in how we spend time, money, and energy. We evolve by what we say in our self-talk and how we interpret what happens around us. We are responsible for our own happiness and fulfillment.

Each of us has secret selves, sometimes secreted even *from ourselves*. By dreaming back our lives and making friends with our own minds, we can know our secret selves.

## NURTURING YOUR SELF

Making changes is one thing. Sticking with our new ways, interests, or disciplines is often another. We all know of people who return from workshops and retreats excited and enthusiastic about their newly found ideals. They have changed their diets and their thinking. They have a new vocabulary and new friends and a fresh perspective.

And then, like all of us, they slip back into the old habits, the old ruts.

Change is not easy. Changing your habits is hard enough. Changing your life requires tenacity and nurturing the new and fragile self emerging like a delicate flower from its bud or a butterfly from its cocoon.

As you are making changes in your life, take time out to do things that will allow you to reflect, refuel, and reconnect. Write in a journal, spend some time in nature, volunteer, find a mentor, join a support group, do some arts and crafts, rent your favorite movie, write a letter, exercise. When you nurture yourself you are also nurturing your dreams.

> Here is the test to find whether your mission on earth is finished. If you're alive, it isn't.
>
> —Richard Bach

## DREAMS INTO ACTION

1. What is the vision of your future?

2. List the ways that you nurture yourself.

3. What self-nurturing would you like to add?

4. While reading this book, what did you find the most difficult? Why? What does this tell you about yourself?

5. What ideas or emotions lingered with you the most?

6. While reading this book, what dreams did you have? What do they tell you?

7. Before going to bed tonight, skim through this book. Then ask for a dream tonight to bring the concepts of this book into a personal focus for you.

# SUGGESTED FURTHER READING

## Chapter 2: Pivotal Dreams

Krakow, Barry, and Joseph Neidhardt. 1992. *Conquering Bad Dreams and Nightmares.* Berkley.

Sendak, Maurice. 1991. *Where the Wild Things Are.* HarperTrophy.

Siegel, Alan. 1990. *Dreams That Can Change Your Life.* Berkley.

————, and Kelly Bulkeley. 1998. *Dreamcatching: Every Parent's Guide to Exploring and Understanding Children's Dreams and Nightmares.* Three Rivers Press.

Ullman, Montague, and Nan Zimmerman. 1979. *Working with Dreams.* Tarcher/Perigee.

## Chapter 4: Childhood Dreams

Feinstein, David, and Stanley Krippner. 1988. *Personal Mythology: Using Ritual, Dreams, and Imagination to Discover Your Inner Story.* Tarcher/Perigee.

Kalweit, Holger. 1988. *Dreamtime and Inner Space: The World of the Shaman.* Shambhala.

LaBerge, Stephen. 1985. *Lucid Dreaming: The Power of Being Awake and Aware in Your Dreams.* Ballantine Books.

Siegel, Alan. 1990. *Dreams That Can Change Your Life.* Berkley.

————, and Kelly Bulkeley. 1998. *Dreamcatching: Every Parent's Guide to Exploring and Understanding Children's Dreams and Nightmares.* Three Rivers Press.

## Chapter 5: Dream Signposts and Endings

Adams, Kathleen. 1990. *Journal to the Self: Twenty-Two Paths to Personal Growth.* Warner Books.

Delaney, Gayle. 1991. *Breakthrough Dreaming.* Bantam Books.

————. 1994. *Sexual Dreams.* Fawcett Columbine.

Faraday, Ann. 1974. *The Dream Game.* Perennial/Harper & Row.

## Chapter 6: Conscious Dreaming

Gackenbach, Jayne, and Stephen LaBerge, editors. 1988. *Conscious Mind, Sleeping Brain: Perspectives on Lucid Dreaming.* Plenum Press.

Harary, Keith, and Pamela Weintraub. 1989. *Lucid Dreams in 30 Days: The Creative Sleep Program.* St. Martin's Press.

LaBerge, Stephen. 1985. *Lucid Dreaming: The Power of Being Awake and Aware in Your Dreams.* Ballantine Books.

————, and Howard Rheingold. 1990. *Exploring the World of Lucid Dreaming.* Ballantine Books.

## Chapter 7: When I Grow Up . . .

Hillman, James. 1988. *The Soul's Code: In Search of Character and Calling.* Random House.

Lerner, Harriet. 1993. *The Dance of Deception.* HarperPerennial.

Moore, Thomas. 1992. *Care of the Soul: A Guide for Cultivating Depth and Sacredness in Everyday Life.* HarperCollins.

## Chapter 8: Daydreams, Fantasies, and Imagination

Bly, Robert. 1988. *A Little Book on the Human Shadow.* HarperSanFrancisco.

Kornfield, Jack. 1993. *A Path with Heart: A Guide Through the Perils and Promises of Spiritual Life.* Bantam Books.

Langs, Robert. 1995. *The Daydream Workbook: Learning the Art of Decoding Your Daydreams.* Alliance.

Person, Ethel. 1995. *By Force of Fantasy.* Penguin Books.

Roth, Geneen. 1982. *Feeding the Hungry Heart: The Experience of Compulsive Eating.* Signet.

Zweig, Connie, and Jeremiah Abrams, editors. 1991. *Meeting the Shadow: The Hidden Power of the Dark Side of Human Nature.* Tarcher/Putnam.

## Chapter 9: Creative Visualization and Guided Imagery

Gawain, Shakti. 1983. *Creative Visualization.* Bantam Books.

Johnson, Robert. 1986. *Inner Work.* HarperSanFrancisco.

————. 1991. *Owning Your Own Shadow: Understanding the Dark Side of the Psyche.* HarperSanFrancisco.

Kornfield, Jack. 1993. *A Path with Heart: A Guide Through the Perils and Promises of Spiritual Life.* Bantam Books.

Mariechild, Diane. 1981. *Mother Wit.* Crossing Press.

Starhawk. 1979. *The Spiral Dance.* HarperSanFrancisco.

## Chapter 10: Waking Nightmares: Crisis and Trauma

Bandler, Richard, and John Grinder. 1982. *ReFraming: Neuro Linguistic Programming and the Transformation of Meaning.* Real People Press.

Carlson, Richard. 1997. *Don't Sweat the Small Stuff.* Hyperion.

Goleman, Daniel. 1995. *Emotional Intelligence.* Bantam Books.

Grof, Stanislav, and Christina Grof, editors. 1989. *Spiritual Emergency: When Personal Transformation Becomes a Crisis.* Tarcher/Perigee.

Hillman, James. 1988. *The Soul's Code: In Search of Character and Calling.* Random House.

Peele, Stanton. 1995. *Diseasing of America.* Lexington Books/Free Press.

Rubin, Lillian. 1996. *The Transcendent Child: Tales of Triumph over the Past.* Basic Books.

Seligman, Martin. 1990. *Learned Optimism: How to Change Your Mind and Your Life.* Pocket Books.

Siebert, Al. 1996. *The Survivor Personality: Why Some People Are Stronger,*

*Smarter and More Skillful at Handling Life's Difficulties . . . and How You Can Be Too.* Perigee.

## Chapter 11: Self-Expression and Self-Talk

Cameron, Julia. 1992. *The Artist's Way: A Spiritual Path to Higher Creativity.* Tarcher/Perigee.

Covey, Stephen. 1990. *The 7 Habits of Highly Effective People.* Fireside/Simon & Schuster.

Fox, John. 1995. *Finding What You Didn't Lose: Expressing Your Truth and Creativity through Poem-Making.* Tarcher/Putnam.

Goulston, Mark, and Philip Goldberg. 1996. *Get Out of Your Own Way: Overcoming Self-Defeating Behavior.* Perigee.

Kurtz, Ernest, and Katherine Ketcham. 1992. *The Spirituality of Imperfection.* Bantam Books.

Metzger, Deena. 1992. *Writing for Your Life: A Guide and Companion to the Inner Worlds.* HarperSanFrancisco.

Smith, Manuel. 1975. *When I Say No, I Feel Guilty.* Bantam Books.

Whitfield, Charles. 1993. *Boundaries and Relationships.* Health Communications.

## Chapter 12: Finding Your Purpose

Boldt, Laurence. 1996. *How to Find the Work You Love.* Arkana.

Buchholtz, Ester Schaler. 1997. *The Call of Solitude: Alonetime in a World of Attachment.* Simon & Schuster.

Gardner, Howard. 1983. *Frames of Mind: The Theory of Multiple Intelligences.* Basic Books.

Gelb, Michael. 1998. *How to Think Like Leonardo da Vinci: Seven Steps to Genius Every Day.* Delacorte Press.

Levoy, Gregg. 1997. *Callings: Finding and Following an Authentic Life.* Harmony Books.

Sher, Barbara. 1979. *Wishcraft.* Ballantine Books.

————. 1994. *I Could Do Anything If I Only Knew What It Was.* Dell.

Simon, Sidney, Leland Howe, and Howard Kirschenbaum. 1995. *Values Clarification: A Practical, Action-Directed Workbook.* Warner Books.

Smith, Hyrum. 1994. *The 10 Natural Laws of Successful Time and Life Management*. Warner Books.

## Chapter 13: First Steps and Strategies

Bandler, Richard, and John Grinder. 1979. *Frogs into Princes: Neuro-Linguistic Programming*. Real People Press.

————. 1982. *ReFraming: Neuro-Linguistic Programming and the Transformation of Meaning*. Real People Press.

Chandler, Steve. 1996. *100 Ways to Motivate Yourself: Change Your Life Forever*. Career Press.

Covey, Stephen. 1990. *The 7 Habits of Highly Effective People*. Fireside/Simon & Schuster.

Fritz, Robert. 1989. *The Path of Least Resistance: Learning to Become a Creative Force in Your Own Life*. Fawcett Columbine.

Kim, Sang H. 1996. *1001 Ways to Motivate Yourself and Others*. Turtle Press.

Lakein, Alan. 1973. *How to Get Control of Your Time and Your Life*. Signet.

Simon, Sidney. 1988. *Getting Unstuck: Breaking Through Your Barriers to Change*. Warner Books.

## Chapter 14: Writing a Mission Statement

Covey, Stephen. 1990. *The 7 Habits of Highly Effective People*. Fireside/Simon & Schuster.

————, A. R. Merrill, and R. R. Merrill. 1994. *First Things First*. Fireside/Simon & Schuster.

Jones, Laurie Beth. 1996. *The Path: Creating Your Mission Statement*. Hyperion.

## Chapter 15: Conclusion: Dream Back Your Life

Anderson, Walter Truett. 1997. *The Future of the Self: Inventing the Postmodern Person*. Tarcher/Putnam.

Gelb, Michael. 1998. *How to Think Like Leonardo da Vinci: Seven Steps to Genius Every Day*. Delacorte Press.

Goldberg, Natalie. 1993. *Long Quiet Highway*. Bantam Books.

Goulston, Mark, and Philip Goldberg. 1996. *Get Out of Your Own Way: Overcoming Self-Defeating Behavior.* Perigee.

Walsh, Roger, and Frances Vaughan, editors. 1993. *Paths Beyond Ego: The Transpersonal Vision.* Tarcher/Putnam.

# BIBLIOGRAPHY

Adams, Cass, editor. 1996. *The Soul Unearthed: Celebrating Wildness and Personal Renewal through Nature.* Tarcher/Putnam.

Adams, Kathleen. 1990. *Journal to the Self: Twenty-Two Paths to Personal Growth.* Warner Books.

Anderson, Walter Truett. 1990. *Reality Isn't What It Used to Be.* Harper-SanFrancisco.

———. 1996. *Evolution Isn't What It Used to Be: The Augmented Animal and the Whole Wired World.* Freeman.

———. 1997. *The Future of the Self: Inventing the Postmodern Person.* Tarcher/Putnam.

Andreas, Steve, and Connirae Andreas. 1987. *Change Your Mind and Keep the Change.* Real People Press.

Aron, Elaine. 1996. *The Highly Sensitive Person: How to Thrive When the World Overwhelms You.* Broadway Books.

Bandler, Richard, and John Grinder. 1979. *Frogs into Princes: Neuro-Linguistic Programming.* Real People Press.

———. 1982. *ReFraming: Neuro-Linguistic Programming and the Transformation of Meaning.* Real People Press.

Barron, Frank, Alfonso Montuori, and Anthea Barron. 1997. *Creators on Creating: Awakening and Cultivating the Imaginative Mind.* Tarcher/Putnam.

Becker, Ernest. 1972. *The Birth and Death of Meaning: An Interdisciplinary Perspective on the Problem of Man.* Free Press.

Bettelheim, Bruno. 1976. *The Uses of Enchantment.* Knopf.

Blanchard, Kenneth, and Norman Vincent Peale. 1988. *The Power of Ethical Management.* Fawcett Columbine.

Bly, Robert. 1988. *A Little Book on the Human Shadow.* HarperSanFrancisco.

Boldt, Laurence. 1996. *How to Find the Work You Love.* Arkana.

Buchholtz, Ester Schaler. 1997. *The Call of Solitude: Alonetime in a World of Attachment.* Simon & Schuster.

Cameron, Julia. 1992. *The Artist's Way: A Spiritual Path to Higher Creativity.* Tarcher/Perigee.

Carlson, Richard. 1997. *Don't Sweat the Small Stuff.* Hyperion.

————, and Benjamin Shield, editors. 1989. *Healers on Healing.* Tarcher/Putnam.

Chandler, Steve. 1996. *100 Ways to Motivate Yourself: Change Your Life Forever.* Career Press.

Covey, Stephen. 1990. *The 7 Habits of Highly Effective People.* Fireside/Simon & Schuster.

————, A. R. Merrill, and R. R. Merrill. 1994. *First Things First.* Fireside/Simon & Schuster.

Csikszentmihalyi, Mihaly. 1990. *Flow: The Psychology of Optimal Experience.* HarperPerennial.

————. 1993. *The Evolving Self: A Psychology for the Third Millennium.* HarperPerennial.

————. 1996. *Creativity: Flow and the Psychology of Discovery and Invention.* HarperCollins.

Daloz, Laurent. 1986. *Effective Teaching and Mentoring: Realizing the Transformational Power of Adult Learning Experiences.* Jossey-Bass.

DeBono, Edward. 1985. *Six Thinking Hats.* Little, Brown.

Delaney, Gayle. 1991. *Breakthrough Dreaming.* Bantam Books.

————. 1994. *Sexual Dreams.* Fawcett Columbine.

Dodson, Betty. 1996. *Sex for One: The Joy of Selfloving.* Crown.

Epel, Naomi. 1993. *Writers Dreaming.* Carol Southern Books.

Faraday, Ann. 1974. *The Dream Game.* Perennial/Harper & Row.

Feinstein, David, and Stanley Krippner. 1988. *Personal Mythology: Using*

*Ritual, Dreams, and Imagination to Discover Your Inner Story.* Tarcher/Perigee.

Foster, Steven, and Meredith Little. 1992. *The Book of the Vision Quest: Personal Transformation in the Wilderness.* Fireside/Simon & Schuster.

Fox, John. 1995. *Finding What You Didn't Lose: Expressing Your Truth and Creativity Through Poem-Making.* Tarcher/Putnam.

———. 1997. *Poetic Medicine: The Healing Art of Poem-Making.* Tarcher/Putnam.

Fritz, Robert. 1989. *The Path of Least Resistance: Learning to Become a Creative Force in Your Own Life.* Fawcett Columbine.

Fritz, Roger. 1993. *Sleep Disorders.* National Sleep Alert.

Gackenbach, Jayne, and Stephen LaBerge, editors. 1988. *Conscious Mind, Sleeping Brain: Perspectives on Lucid Dreaming.* Plenum Press.

Gallegos, Eligio. 1985. *The Personal Totem Pole.* Moon Bear Press.

Gardner, Howard. 1983. *Frames of Mind: The Theory of Multiple Intelligences.* Basic Books.

Garfield, Patricia. 1974. *Creative Dreaming.* Ballantine.

Gawain, Shakti. 1983. *Creative Visualization.* Bantam Books.

Gelb, Michael. 1998. *How to Think Like Leonardo da Vinci: Seven Steps to Genius Every Day.* Delacorte Press.

Gendlin, Eugene. 1986. *Let Your Body Interpret Your Dreams.* Chiron.

Goldberg, Natalie. 1986. *Writing Down the Bones.* Shambhala.

———. 1993. *Long Quiet Highway.* Bantam Books.

Goleman, Daniel. 1995. *Emotional Intelligence.* Bantam Books.

Gough, Russell. 1998. *Character Is Destiny: The Value of Personal Ethics in Everyday Life.* Forum/Prima.

Goulston, Mark, and Philip Goldberg. 1996. *Get Out of Your Own Way: Overcoming Self-Defeating Behavior.* Perigee.

Grof, Stanislav, and Christina Grof, editors. 1989. *Spiritual Emergency: When Personal Transformation Becomes a Crisis.* Tarcher/Perigee.

Harary, Keith, and Pamela Weintraub. 1989. *Lucid Dreams in 30 Days: The Creative Sleep Program.* St. Martin's Paperbacks.

Harner, Michael. 1990. *The Way of the Shaman.* HarperSanFrancisco.

Heinlein, Robert A. 1973. *The Notebooks of Lazarus Long: Aphorisms from "Time Enough for Love."* Putnam.

Helmstetter, Shad. 1982. *What to Say When You Talk to Yourself.* Pocket Books/Simon & Schuster.

Hendricks, Gay, and Kathlyn Hendricks. 1990. *Conscious Loving: The Journey to Co-Commitment.* Bantam Books.

Hendrix, Harville. 1988. *Getting the Love You Want.* HarperPerennial.

———. 1992. *Keeping the Love You Find.* Pocket Books.

Hillman, James. 1988. *The Soul's Code: In Search of Character and Calling.* Random House.

———, and Michael Ventura. 1992. *We've Had a Hundred Years of Psychotherapy and the World's Getting Worse.* HarperSanFransciso.

Hoyt, Michael. 1995. *Brief Therapy and Managed Care.* Jossey-Bass.

Johnson, Robert. 1986. *Inner Work.* HarperSanFrancisco.

———. 1991. *Owning Your Own Shadow: Understanding the Dark Side of the Psyche.* HarperSanFrancisco.

Jones, Laurie Beth. 1996. *The Path: Creating Your Mission Statement.* Hyperion.

Jung, Carl. 1989. *Memories, Dreams, Reflections.* Vintage Books.

Kalweit, Holger. 1988. *Dreamtime and Inner Space: The World of the Shaman.* Shambhala.

Kegan, Robert. 1982. *The Evolving Self: Problem and Process in Human Development.* Harvard University Press.

———. 1994. *In Over Our Heads: The Mental Demands of Modern Life.* Harvard University Press.

Kidder, Rushworth M. 1995. *How Good People Make Tough Choices: Resolving the Dilemmas of Ethical Living.* Fireside/Simon & Schuster

Kim, Sang H. 1996. *1001 Ways to Motivate Yourself and Others.* Turtle Press.

Kornfield, Jack. 1993. *A Path with Heart: A Guide Through the Perils and Promises of Spiritual Life.* Bantam Books.

Krakow, Barry, and Joseph Neidhardt. 1992. *Conquering Bad Dreams and Nightmares.* Berkley.

Kryger, Meir, Thomas Roth, and William Dement. 1994. *Principles and Practices of Sleep Medicine,* 2nd edition. Saunders.

Kurtz, Ernest, and Katherine Ketcham. 1992. *The Spirituality of Imperfection.* Bantam Books.

LaBerge, Stephen. 1985. *Lucid Dreaming: The Power of Being Awake and Aware in Your Dreams.* Ballantine Books.

————, and Howard Rheingold. 1990. *Exploring the World of Lucid Dreaming.* Ballantine Books.

Lakein, Alan. 1973. *How to Get Control of Your Time and Your Life.* Signet.

Lamott, Anne. 1994. *Bird by Bird: Some Instructions on Writing and Life.* Anchor/Doubleday.

Langs, Robert. 1995. *The Daydream Workbook: Learning the Art of Decoding Your Daydreams.* Alliance.

Lerner, Harriet. 1989. *The Dance of Intimacy.* HarperPerennial.

————. 1993. *The Dance of Deception.* HarperPerennial.

————. 1997. *The Dance of Anger.* HarperPerennial.

Levoy, Gregg. 1997. *Callings: Finding and Following an Authentic Life.* Harmony Books.

Loftus, Elizabeth, and Katherine Ketchum. 1994. *The Myth of Repressed Memory.* St. Martin's Press.

Maisel, Eric. 1995. *Fearless Creating.* Tarcher/Putnam.

————. 1999. *Deep Writing.* Tarcher/Putnam.

Mariechild, Diane. 1981. *Mother Wit.* Crossing Press.

Maslow, Abraham. 1962. *Toward a Psychology of Being.* Van Nostrand.

————. 1971. *The Farther Reaches of Human Nature.* Esalen/Viking.

Mazza, Joan. 1998. *Dreaming Your Real Self: A Personal Approach to Dream Interpretation.* Perigee/Putnam.

Metzger, Deena. 1992. *Writing for Your Life: A Guide and Companion to the Inner Worlds.* HarperSanFrancisco.

Moore, Thomas. 1992. *Care of the Soul: A Guide for Cultivating Depth and Sacredness in Everyday Life.* HarperCollins.

Nelson, John, and Andrea Nelson. 1996. *Sacred Sorrows: Embracing and Transforming Depression.* Tarcher/Putnam.

Orsborn, Carol. 1997. *The Art of Resilience: 100 Paths to Wisdom and Strength in an Uncertain World.* Three Rivers Press.

Palmer, Helen, editor. 1998. *Inner Knowing: Consciousness, Creativity, Insight, Intuition.* Tarcher/Putnam.

Peele, Stanton. 1995. *Diseasing of America.* Lexington Books/Free Press.

Perkins, John. 1990. *PsychoNavigation: Techniques for Travel Beyond Time.* Destiny Books.

————. 1994. *The World Is As You Dream It: Shamanic Teachings from the Amazon and Andes*. Destiny Books.

————. 1997. *Shapeshifting: Shamanic Techniques for Global and Personal Transformation*. Destiny Books.

Perry, Susan K. 1999. *Writing in Flow: Keys to Enhanced Creativity*. Writer's Digest Books.

Person, Ethel S. 1996. *By Force of Fantasy*. Penguin Books.

Roth, Gabrielle. 1989. *Maps to Ecstasy: Teachings of an Urban Shaman*. Nataraj.

Roth, Geneen. 1982. *Feeding the Hungry Heart: The Experience of Compulsive Eating*. Signet.

Rubin, Lillian. 1996. *The Transcendent Child: Tales of Triumph over the Past*. Basic Books.

Seligman, Martin. 1990. *Learned Optimism: How to Change Your Mind and Your Life*. Pocket Books.

Sher, Barbara. 1979. *Wishcraft*. Ballantine Books.

————. 1994. *I Could Do Anything If I Only Knew What It Was*. Dell.

Siebert, Al. 1996. *The Survivor Personality: Why Some People Are Stronger, Smarter, and More Skillful at Handling Life's Difficulties . . . and How You Can Be, Too*. Perigee.

Siegel, Alan. 1990. *Dreams That Can Change Your Life*. Berkley.

————, and Kelly Bulkeley. 1998. *Dreamcatching: Every Parent's Guide to Exploring and Understanding Children's Dreams and Nightmares*. Three Rivers Press.

Simon, Sidney. 1988. *Getting Unstuck: Breaking Through Your Barriers to Change*. Warner Books.

————, Leland Howe, and Howard Kirschenbaum. 1995. *Values Clarification: A Practical, Action-Directed Workbook*. Warner Books.

Sinetar, Marsha. 1987. *Do What You Love, the Money Will Follow: Discovering Your Right Livelihood*. Dell.

Smith, Hyrum. 1994. *The 10 Natural Laws of Successful Time and Life Management*. Warner Books.

Smith, Manuel. 1975. *When I Say No, I Feel Guilty*. Bantam Books.

Starhawk. 1979. *The Spiral Dance*. HarperSanFrancisco.

Stevens, Jose, and Lena Stevens. 1988. *Secrets of Shamanism: Tapping the Spirit Power Within You*. Avon Books.

Tart, Charles, editor. 1969. *Altered States of Consciousness*. Doubleday Anchor.

————. 1987. *Waking Up*. Shambhala.

————. 1989. *Open Mind, Discriminating Mind: Reflections on Human Possibilities*. Harper & Row.

————. 1994. *Living the Mindful Life*. Shambhala.

Tavris, Carol. 1989. *Anger: The Misunderstood Emotion*. Touchstone/Simon & Schuster.

————. 1992. *The Mismeasure of Woman*. Touchstone/Simon & Schuster.

Taylor, Jeremy. 1983. *Dreamwork*. Paulist Press.

————. 1992. *Where People Fly and Water Runs Uphill*. Warner Books.

Tedeschi, Richard, and Lawrence Calhoun. 1995. *Trauma and Transformation: Growing in the Aftermath of Suffering*. Sage.

Torrey, E. Fuller. 1983. *The Mind Game: Witchdoctors and Psychiatrists*. Jason Aronson.

Ullman, Montague. 1996. *Appreciating Dreams*. Sage.

————, and Nan Zimmerman. 1979. *Working with Dreams*. Tarcher/Perigee.

Van De Castle, Robert. 1994. *Our Dreaming Mind*. Ballantine Books.

Ventura, Michael. 1993. *Letters at 3 A.M.: Reports on Endarkenment*. Spring.

Walsh, Roger. 1990. *The Spirit of Shamanism*. Tarcher/Perigee.

————, and Frances Vaughan, editors. 1993. *Paths Beyond Ego: The Transpersonal Vision*. Tarcher/Putnam.

Weiner-Davis, Michele. 1995. *Change Your Life and Everyone in It*. Fireside/Simon & Schuster.

White, Michael, and David Epston. 1990. *Narrative Means to Therapeutic Ends*. Norton.

Whitfield, Charles. 1993. *Boundaries and Relationships*. Health Communications.

Yapko, Michael. 1997. *Breaking the Patterns of Depression*. Main Street Books.

Zweig, Connie, and Jeremiah Abrams, editors. 1991. *Meeting the Shadow: The Hidden Power of the Dark Side of Human Nature*. Tarcher/Putnam.

————, and Steve Wolf. 1997. *Romancing the Shadow: Illuminating the Dark Side of the Soul*. Ballantine.

# INDEX

*Photo by Richard Nathanson*

Joan Mazza is the author of *Dreaming Your Real Self: A Personal Approach to Dream Interpretation* and *Dream Back Your Life: A Practical Guide to Dreams, Daydreams, and Fantasies.* She is a psychotherapist and licensed mental health counselor, holds a master's degree in counseling psychology, and conducts ongoing groups in South Florida as well as national seminars. She teaches a variety of other topics including:

• How to Say No With a Smile: Setting Personal Boundaries

• Managing Your Emotions

• When Life Gives You Lemons . . .

• Conscious Sexuality

• Motivate Yourself!

As a speaker, Joan Mazza brings seminars to both professionals and the public, addressing the concerns and frustrations of people in "midlife" crises regardless of age. With humor and personal anecdotes, she invites people to be themselves, take risks, and dream back their lives. She is a past president of The Book Group of South Florida, an organization of authors and book industry professionals. Her short stories, articles, poetry, and essays have appeared in many publications.

She lives in Fort Lauderdale, Florida, with her two poodles, Bambi and Razz-ma-Tazz.

(954) 564-6621

fax (954) 564-0001

Toll-free (888) DREAM-30

http://www.joanmazza.com